THE BOY

WITH

STRIPES

REV. EDDIE WIGGINS
Yashewa is Lord Ministries

ISBN: 978-1-60383-291-5

Published by:
Holy Fire Publishing
717 Old Trolley Road
Attn: Suite 6, Publishing Unit #116
Summerville, SC 29485

www.ChristianPublish.com

Printed in the United States of America and the United Kingdom

PREFACE

In all the horror, God kept me.

Through all the tribulations, Jesus was at my side. After reading the scribbled notes of this story, my Pastor told me that God's hand was always upon me, even as a small child, shielding me and protecting my life, even though I did not know Him. I barely knew of Him, yet He kept me. Yes, I suffered greatly; but Jesus kept me alive. Through it all, Jesus kept my mind, body, spirit, and soul.

As I went through it all, I was totally unaware.

I was totally unaware of His presence, but He kept me for a day and a time that is now.

I give God all the Glory, all the Praise, and all the Honor. I thank God that He made it possible for you to read this book.

I pray that you will go past the horror to see the Mighty and Loving God we serve.

I couldn't at that time, but I do now.

Always here,

Rev. Eddie
Yashewa is Lord Ministries

THANKS AND ACKNOWLEDGEMENTS

I want to thank my Lord and Savior Jesus Christ for saving my life and soul. Thank you Lord Jesus for all you have ever done for me, all you are doing, and all you plan to do.

I want to thank my Pastor. You are truly a Shepherd after God's own heart!!

Ed Potter, you are incredible!! You never cease to amaze me. Thank you for all of your help and support and many hours of sweat and hard work to make this book possible.

I thank God for the Heavenly Handymen. I also want to thank each and every Blunt. You knew me, and put up with me when I was at my worst. I pray that your knowing me now will be a blessing to you.

Mama Anderson, I love you. Eddie and Christina, you are the best! Lee, I'm so proud of you. Angelina and Gilbert, you have my heart, and I love you so very much. And to my dad, I love you. Sis, you are an inspiration, and I love you so much. I will always be here for you. Herb, I love you too.

I want to thank all of my editors that God has so anointed and sent to this ministry to bless this work. Thank you so much Joyce McHugh, you are so good at what you do and have really blessed this work with your expertise and professionalism. Loretta Walker, thank you for all your support and encouragement. God is truly using you to bless this Ministry and I thank you for all of your hard work and the many blessings you have given so unselfishly to this Ministry.

Minister Cynthia Blas, your work and anointing are invaluable to this work and Ministry. Thank you so much for your many hours of making this work as fine as it is. Ed Potter, you started this editing before the Lord sent us all these professionals. Thanks again. You have worn so many "hats" in this Ministry.

Thank you so much Roderick Gray for your contributions in my life and toward this book. You knew me when I was at my worst. You saw me and still put up with me. (Smile) You not only named this book, but you also helped with the back cover! God is truly using you and it is a great pleasure to watch. Much love, my brother! God bless you Christian. Keep up the good work. Before Angelina, there was you. I love you, Chris, and I am so proud of you and how you have grown.

I also want to thank the Howard University for the use of the picture of Dr. Drew on page 14.

The proceeds from this book will go to the building of the

Kingdom of God—the youth programs, ministries, and missions that God has put in my heart: the children behind bars, Aim High, my church, and my ministry—Yashewa is Lord Ministries—for the spreading of the Gospel. No proceeds shall be used on any types of luxury items. Know in your heart that you won't see me driving a Rolls Royce or any other expensive car, while God's children are hungry and homeless. I thank God that I am not into things and stuff. There is nothing I want more than to help others, fill the needs of those in need, and the salvation of souls. May God's will be done, not mine. In the Mighty Name of Jesus.

Table of Contents

CHAPTER 1: MY FIRST MEMORY

I was born into this world on April 30, 1955 in Riverside, California. At least that's what I was told by my adoptive parents. My adoptive dad, who I will refer to as Dad, told me that there was an adoption agency on the corner of Arlington Avenue and Adams Boulevard. I believe he called it the West Adams Adoption Agency, but I could be mistaken. He told me that I was adopted at the age of two; so that means that, in 1957, they brought me home.

My first memory was of being knocked over in my high chair for refusing to eat a banana. I've noticed that babies sometimes throw food, so perhaps I threw the banana down, or just refused to eat it. Whatever I did caused my adoptive mom, who I will refer to as Mom, to hit me so hard that my high chair toppled over and fell with me in it. I can remember how slowly it started to topple, and I remember feeling the tray tight against me, holding me in so I couldn't escape. I really got hurt when I hit the floor, but she left me crying on the floor as she screamed at me before leaving the room.

A great memory to start this life, eh? I remember that we lived in an apartment on Adams Boulevard. It had an incredibly large front yard with lots of grass and a path on the side of the building, with cement stairs which led to the back. I remember playing on the grass and running up and down this path. This is where they started—the beatings Mom would give me.

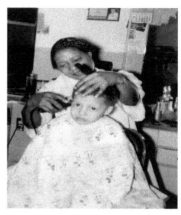

Eddie in a wagon, and in the barber's chair

It seemed that everything I did was wrong and, in return, I was punished with a beating. She would hit me with her hands or with a belt. Let's not forget, I was only two years old—too young to know what was going on, and too young to hate. I didn't like her at all. In fact, I feared her.

Then we moved to a huge house on a hill. The house was so big that it scared me. I remember Mom telling someone it was 1957. The area was Windsor Hills, right behind Baldwin Hills. I remember Mom saying that, when she went to look at the house, the realtor slammed the door in her face and said, "No coloreds!"

My mom didn't take to that sort of treatment. She was an educated woman: a teacher and student counselor. (I always wondered why I was treated so badly by a woman who was trained to help children!)

Mom was dark-skinned, but my dad was a light-skinned black man who was adopted, like me, but by a white family. This was in Omaha, Nebraska, where his dad was a doctor, and so was his dad's brother. My dad became a famous surgeon after studying under Dr. Charles Drew. Today you can see my dad in an American Red Cross ad for famous black Americans. He is standing next to Dr. Charles Drew during an examination of a patient, with other residents and medical staff.

Charles Richard Drew (1904-50) was an African-American physician in Washington, D.C. A surgeon and a professor at Howard University, he developed a means of preserving blood plasma for transfusion. During World War II he headed the program that sent blood to Great Britain and was the director of the first American Red Cross Blood Bank.

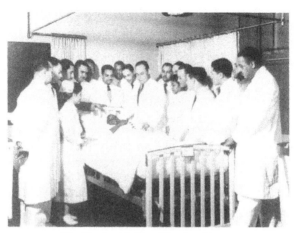

My Dad with Dr. Charles Drew

I loved my dad because I felt protected when he was around. When he was home, I didn't get beaten by Mom.

Anyway, back to the open house at 4154 Olympiad Drive. After the realtor said, "No coloreds" and slammed the door in my mom's face, she returned to the open house, but with a lawyer, and she *bought* that house! It was a huge house that sometimes creaked at night. There were so many rooms that it scared me.

Mom asked me, "Do you like it?"

I told her, "No! It's too big and too scary!"

She said, "Well, this is where rich people live, and this will be our home, so get used to it."

When I took my first bath in that big ol' house, even though the water was warm, the air was so cold, it gave me goose pimples. As I was bathing, the drips from the faucet were echoing so loud, that it frightened me.

Almost immediately after moving in, the beatings really started on a regular basis, every day. It seemed I would always say or do something wrong and get punished for it with a beating. And then I started getting beaten with a razor strop— a three-foot long strap of leather, three to four inches wide, that is usually attached to the side of a barber's chair to sharpen single-edged razors. When used to strike the tender skin of a child, it leaves behind a wide red welt just about ready to bleed. A second strike in that same area might cause blood to squirt out and splash the ceiling and walls.

Mom told me that, if I showed my cut up, scabby, back to anyone or told anyone, especially my dad, about these beatings, she would *kill* me. I believed her because of the things she said to me and the way she was beating me.

Even if I obeyed her, I knew that one day she would kill me anyway. Some of the more lovely things she'd say to me were, "I hate you, and wish you were dead!" "We never should have adopted you!" "I wish we could take you back to that adoption agency, you bastard!" "I wish you would go somewhere and die." "You are sick! Something's wrong with you. No wonder your parents didn't want you!"

Eddie on his trike

By the age of four or five, I had been taught how to hate. Passionately. With feeling. With imagination. With murder in my heart.

In 1959, when I was four, Mom and Dad had their first natural child. They never hit him or talked down to him. He was their perfect child: everything they wanted in a child; everything that I wasn't—that was my little brother Herbert.

CHAPTER 2: I LIVED TO SEE MY FIFTH BIRTHDAY

When I was five, I went to the Mary Clay Preschool. The store next door had boxes of fruit outside on tables. When Mom dropped me off, I always asked her if we could go there, but she always said no. One day, I left the school and went next door to the store and grabbed an orange, then went back to school. I knew nothing about money or buying things, so I had no idea that I had just "stolen" that orange. A man from the store came to the school and started yelling at me, so one of the teachers called my mom. She picked me up, put me in the car, beat me something terrible, and I never went back to that school.

This incident started the "go upstairs, take your clothes off, get wet in the tub, stand there, and wait for me." She had found a new love! Whipping the snot out of me wet. It really stung, and the blood would squirt a lot farther. Keep in mind that I was only five years old. I wasn't allowed out of the backyard. I had no friends. I wasn't allowed to have any TV, radio, or have anyone to talk to…or to tell. Standing there dripping wet, cold, frightened, scared of even my own shadow while waiting for that razor strop, I felt so all alone, so unwanted, and so full of hate; but I didn't dare show it. The pain was overwhelming, and blood would spray with each swing of that razor strop. I'd scream, hoping it would soon stop, but it never stopped soon enough for me. Ten, twenty, or sometimes thirty swings later she would finally stop, leaving me a welted, bloody mess.

I cried every night. And I prayed. Since we went to the nearby Episcopal Church on Sundays, I'd heard of God, and every night I prayed that he would kill Mom. "If there is a God," I'd say, "please kill her before she kills me!"

At six or seven years of age, it's so hard to comprehend death. What would become of me? I wanted so much to love and be loved. I was so afraid of dying, but every night, I would think about what it would be like to be dead, and scare myself even more.

When I was allowed to watch TV, I'd watch family shows like the Brady Bunch or the Partridge Family and wonder to myself, "Can this be real? What's wrong with my family? How come we don't act like this?" Deep inside, I felt a yearning to love, and God knew how much I wanted to be loved.

My beloved best friend was Mitzi, our standard poodle. She was a big tall poodle and seemed to tower over me. Whenever I got a beating and was thrown into the backyard, Mitzi always comforted me. She licked my face until my tears were gone.

We played all day together sometimes. The best part was that she didn't hate me. Instead, she showed me so much love—as if I were her puppy. She showed me more love in an afternoon, than my mom did her entire life.

A white family lived next door with a little girl named Dee-Dee who wasn't allowed to play with me. I often saw Dee-Dee at her bedroom window, looking down at me in our yard.

One day she asked me, "Are you black or white?" and I answered, "What's that?"

She said, "You know, what are you?" but I had no idea what she was talking about. "Go ask your mom," she said.

My mom was in the kitchen when I approached her and, although hesitant, asked her, "Mom, am I black or white?" and she threw a fit.

"Where did you get that from?" she demanded, so I told her, "Dee-Dee asked me, and I want to know. Dee-Dee told me she was white and that you are black, so what am I?"

My mom slapped me dizzy and told me to get back outside in the backyard and not to talk to Dee-Dee. Of course Dee-Dee was in her window and saw me crying. She asked me, "Well, what are you?" I wiped my tears and told her that I still didn't know and I didn't care to find out either because it hurts too much to ask.

Eddie's grade school photo

CHAPTER 3: MY DAD AND THE CHURCH

My dad was usually gone during the week. His morning hours were spent performing surgeries on people and he wouldn't get home until after dark. Except for Saturdays and Sundays, Wednesdays were my favorite days since he worked only half a day and we would go grocery shopping in the afternoons.

I loved it when he was home because Mom would never beat me when he was around. Saturdays he would take me to the YMCA with my brother. Sundays we would go to church and then go out to eat.

I didn't like our church, but my dad was a deacon there. I really loved hearing him read the Word of God. He was awesome: so eloquent and learned and he never mispronounced a word. So many words that I could never even begin to pronounce flowed like honey from his lips. Except for the communion, this was my favorite part of the service. I was so proud of my dad and the way he could speak the Word of God.

To me, our church was scary, with the choir singing like ghosts and that organ playing music like out of a horror movie. No one was allowed to clap or talk or even move except the altar boys and our priest. A big man who used to sit behind me and sing had the deepest voice that I had ever heard. I learned that his name is Dr. Ed Jordan. He told me not too long ago that I was the little boy who couldn't sit still in church. I told him I still can't. I had every part of the service memorized, except the sermon and the Word my dad would read, so I was bored beyond belief.

I hid the money my dad gave me to put in the offering, and I bought candy from a vending machine outside the room where Sunday school was held after church. Once at Sunday school, during a reading of the Book of Revelation, I asked so many questions that the Sunday school teacher told me to ask Father Quimby for the answers, so I did. He said, "No one can really understand Revelation, so why don't you read something else?"

That broke my heart. I thought, "Well, if he's our leader and even *he* doesn't know, then how will I ever find out what will ever become of me?"

I was about eight or nine and didn't have a Bible of my own. My dad's Bible was too big and I couldn't understand what I was reading in his King James Version. For all I understood, it could have been written in Chinese.

Dad liked things quiet, so we couldn't really ever talk just to talk, or for me to ask my questions; and asking Mom was too painful.

Besides, my hate for her had grown out of control. I would cry myself to sleep at night, plotting and planning for her murder. I felt alone, hated, afraid, beaten down, different from everyone else, and unloved. If anyone touched me, I would jump because of my back. I even hated my own name.

My mom started using flashcards for English and math and, if I gave the wrong answer, she would beat me with that razor strop. The beatings came every day except Wednesdays, Saturdays, and Sundays. On Saturdays, if my dad didn't take me to the YMCA or keep me with him, I would get beaten, so I would beg and cry for him to take me with him. Most of the time he would give in and take me along, but he still didn't know why I was so emphatic about being with him.

CHAPTER 4: MY BABY SISTER

When I was eight, Mom and Dad brought home their second natural child, my sweet little sister Susie Adele Wiggins. She was so precious, so sweet, and so beautiful that I fell in love with her the moment I saw her.

On the day they brought Susie home from the hospital, Mom called my brother and me downstairs to announce, "This is your new baby sister."

We looked at her in amazement and I reached out to touch her. My mom said to me, "You aren't to speak to her, don't even look at her, and if you ever touch her, I will kill you, do you understand?"

"Yes," I said, and went back up to my room.

Wow! To be shot down before you even left the runway! Mom had just torn away my dreams of having a little sister on whom I could pour all this love that was in me. My mother was just pure evil through and through. I thought, "I wish my brother and sister and I could just go somewhere with my dad and never come back."

I think every boy with a younger sister wants to protect her, love her, take her places, show her things, and beat up other boys who say anything against her. I wanted to teach my little sister how to ride bicycles in the hills around our house, how to fly kites, how to build models, and how to play electric football. I wanted to share my life with her and be there for her. My mom would deny me even this? I felt like such an outcast. Worthless, and not good enough.

I really hated Mom for that, and even worse, I hated myself more. She loved my brother and sister, yet hated me so much. I hated me, too! I was always saying something wrong and always did the wrong things, but anything and everything *they* did was perfect in my mother's eyes. As we grew up, they barely spoke to me because she told them I was terrible, and warned them not to be like me.

I used to make believe I was someone else. I wanted so badly to be someone Mom would love instead of hate. Someone she would hold and hug. During my entire childhood, I never got a hug or kiss, a compliment, or an "I'm proud of you." With all of this, you might think that I wanted to die, but quite the opposite: I wanted to live. I wanted to love. And I wanted to *be* loved.

One afternoon in the backyard in the shade of the peach tree, I was playing with some plastic cowboys and Indians. (Of course, my Indians always won.) Mom brought Susie outside in a carrier, put her in the shade under the tree with me, and told me, "Watch her, but don't touch her."

I was elated that Mom trusted me to watch my little sister and, boy, did I watch her. All of a sudden, a leaf fell from the tree and landed on her naked tummy. She giggled and laughed, which I thought was so cute. I laughed, too, and picked up the leaf off her tummy, being careful not to touch her. I dropped it on her tummy again, and she giggled and laughed. Again and again we did this, and laughed together, and then all of a sudden, Mom came storming out of the house screaming, "Get away from her! What are you doing to her!"

I tried to explain that the tree had dropped the leaf.... She grabbed a switch from the tree and smacked me all over my body, cursing me and calling me names, before taking Susie inside.

There I lay in the backyard, crying and bleeding and hurt— and really getting better at hating her and plotting her murder. After that, I planned every day to kill her really, really good. The perfect murder, that was what I was planning. I would kill her and no one would know it was me; and then we could have a great, loving, beautiful family without her.

CHAPTER 5: STILL ALIVE AT TEN

I was ten in 1965 when Mom was watching the Watts Riots on TV. I hid in the hallway behind her, watching in disbelief as people were beaten and shot. Crowds of people were screaming, "Burn, baby, burn!"

She turned around and saw me standing there, and told me to go outside with my brother. We were running around a tree screaming, "Burn, baby, burn!" when my mother came outside. She told me I was a militant and that I would end up dead or in prison. She then beat me with a broom handle in front of my brother.

I decided that day that I wanted to be a Black Panther when I grew up so I could stop the oppression in black neighborhoods. I wanted to feed the hungry and ensure justice for all. I wanted to be a militant hero who my mother would really hate. She hated me now, for no good reason. Let's make sure we give her a really good reason. I would be the best militant ever. To spite *her* of course!

I finally got the nerve to ask my dad's secretary if I was white or black. She explained to me all the different races and colors, racism, prejudice, and hatred, and told me that I looked mixed. She said, "You are probably half black, and half white.

You could also have some Mexican or American Indian in you."

I told her about some of the feelings I already had regarding hate and prejudice, that people should just be what they are and not hate others because they are different. When she told me about Huey Newton and Stokely Carmichael, I said that they were my heroes. Even after she disagreed with me, explaining that they hated white men as much as white men hated blacks, I still secretly made them my childhood heroes. To me, being a child with a limited vision of my future, they were heroic! They took a stand for a people when no one else would. They were willing to die for what they believed: that the black man was being brutalized by the police; and that their neighborhoods and schools and employment opportunities were sub-standard. They wanted true equal rights. My intention was to run away one day to join them.

I guess Mom was right on that one. I did have the desire to be a militant, a desire fueled by my raging fire of hatred toward her. What she didn't know was that, after becoming a Black Panther, she would be my first victim.

One day at school on the playground, the coach was choosing basketball teams. In those days, you were either "skins" or "shirts." Skins had to remove their shirts and play bare-skinned. Shirts left their shirts on. I always had to be shirts, of course, because of the bloody stripes on my back. This day, however, the coach picked me to play on the skins team. I pleaded with him to let me play with my shirt on. He asked, "You always play with the shirts! What's the matter? Are you ashamed of your body? Do you think you are too skinny?"

I refused to take off my shirt. I'm sure he felt disobedience and defiance from me, and he led me away from the other children. As we walked away, he led me by placing his hand on my back, and I cringed in pain and jumped away. When we got behind the bungalows, he asked to see my back.

My heart raced. I knew I shouldn't show him, but I wanted him to understand why I couldn't ever show my back to anyone. I removed my shirt with tears in my eyes and, when he saw my bloody, scars-on-top-of-scars back, he shouted, "My *God*! Who did this to you?!"

I was crying, my face wet with tears. I told him I fell. I looked at his face to see if he believed me. He started crying and fell to his knees and, with tears streaming down his face, asked if my dad had done this to me. I shook my head no as he held me by my arms and looked through his tears into my crying eyes. I told him my dad had never hit me. He wiped the tears from his left cheek and asked me, "Did your mom do this to you? Who did this terrible thing?"

I had never seen a grown man cry before, and part of me wanted to trust him. But most of me wanted to walk away before something happened that would let Mom know that I had told someone what she had been doing to me. I told him through sobs and tears, "No, it wasn't my mom," I lied, but I could no longer look him in his pleading, crying eyes.

He shook me by my arms and told me that no child should have to go through this, and that he would have to report this. He explained that he would have to take pictures, and I would have to go to the hospital. He also said that he would have to notify the police.

My little heart broke and I *really* started crying. I slipped and said, "She will kill me if you tell anyone!"

He said, "*She!?!* You mean your *mother* did this to you? Why did she *do* this? What did *you* do?"

I told him what she would say and do to me, and that sometimes I would say and do things that she didn't like. He asked me to share with him some of those things that would cause her to beat me as she had, so I did. He told me that those were things that *all* children did, and that was no excuse. He told me that she was verbally and physically abusing me, and that there were laws against what she was doing to me.

I told him that he didn't understand. "She told me if I ever tell on her or show anyone my back that she would kill me, and *I believe her!*"

Then I added, "Do you *want* her to kill me?"

"Well, it looks like she's trying to kill you anyway," he replied. I begged and pleaded with him not to tell anyone, and I made him promise. He finally gave in. After he held me for a while, we dried our tears and went back to the playground.

From that day on, I was always shirts.

Going to sleep that night, I thought, "Coach is a nice man. I'm sorry I made him cry." I also remembered him saying, "My *God!* Who did this to you?" I thought, "He knows God, too?"

Everybody else but me seemed to know God. Where *is* God really? I thought I had heard that God sees everything. I wondered if God was watching over me. Could He really see what was happening to me? Why didn't He do anything? Does He hear the cries of a child? Do you have to be a certain age before God will help? If so, it appeared that I wasn't going to make it to that age if Mom had anything to do with it. I had heard one Sunday at church that God was the defender of the weak. I could sure use some defending, Lord. Can you hear me? God? Are you there?

Sleep was always painful, I had to sleep on my stomach. I would awaken in pain if I accidentally rolled over during the night, which would cause my wounds to bleed and my pajama top to eventually stick to the wounds. Peeling off my top the next morning would also peel off the scabs, causing even more pain. I really hated being a kid.

People would say how good life is, but this thing called life wasn't getting along too well with me—a very rocky start, indeed. I wondered, "If life is supposed to be so good, but feels this bad, then I surely don't want to die!"

CHAPTER 6: THE SHERIFF, THE TURNERS, AND LITTLE RED

It wasn't unusual to find me riding my bike in front of the house, my bike with a football in the basket in front. A black sheriff's deputy would park up the street, watching the stop sign, and I would pull up beside him. Sometimes he would get out of his patrol car and play catch with me. He was such a nice man who always had a smile and something nice to say.

A couple of times, he pulled me over on my bike to ask me if we could play catch. A few times, he turned on the lights on top of his cruiser for me. He called them his "bubble gum machine." Boy, I loved to see those lights come on! I'd always ask him to hit the siren, but he almost never did.

He always seemed to be around when I ran through his stop signs, always the four-way stops because I just knew the cross traffic would stop. He hated that, and would chase me down, then really get on my case. "You have to stop running those stop signs! One of these days, somebody's gonna hit you! Do you hear me? I don't want to have to scrape you up off the pavement! Are you listening to me? I know your dad, and I will take you home to tell him. Don't you run my stop signs anymore, you little squirt! Now get outta here!"

He would pretend to be mad at me, but I could see right through him. I think I ran the stop signs mostly just to make his day. He was probably bored beyond belief in our neighborhood anyway. Nothing ever happened.

I promised myself that if Mom ever got close to killing me, I would go to him; but I hadn't told him what was happening to me. I didn't know if he could, or would, be able to help me. I wasn't willing to take the chance that he couldn't.

Just a couple of blocks away from our house, was where Little Red lived. Little Red and I went to Windsor Hills Elementary School together. He was a quiet kid who pretty much stayed to himself. We played some, and he got curious about the red stains showing on the back of my shirt. I told him it was paint. He didn't look like he believed me, but I never showed him.

We liked to play baseball and kickball on the playground together. He was fun to play with, but I avoided him some because he was smarter than the average bear and, given some time, would have figured out my back situation.

One day, he just stopped coming by and he no longer attended Windsor Hills Elementary. Boy, did I ever miss him! Kickball was never the same.

Little Red broke his arm a couple of times and was one of my dad's patients. My dad fixed him like new. Little Red's daddy was the singer Ray Charles, so I guess Little Red was really Little Ray, but everyone called him Little Red. Don't ask me why. Probably his red hair, and many red freckles.

My dad would often listen to Ray Charles records in his den. He liked Ray Charles and so did I. There were a lot of songs that Ray Charles sang that had that country feeling in them. Ray Charles was about the only black artist you could listen to and hear some good ol' country music. I liked the fact that my dad and I had Ray Charles in common.

A lot of stars and entertainers lived in my neighborhood. I went to school with most of their children. I did not know them all personally, but I guess they sure knew me. Or felt the effects of my being there amongst them. I remember the house that Barry Gordy lived in. He may have lost a few sprinkler heads on his front lawn as I screamed by on my bike chasing imaginary bad guys. I was a super hero on my bike you know. Somebody had to keep our neighborhood safe besides my sheriff friend.

Nancy Wilson had a wonderful circle driveway that I attempted to leave skid marks from my tires on, but she told me to get out of her driveway with my bike so I left her driveway alone. I left plenty of skid marks in front of Ray Charles' house though. He lived on a fantastic hill and I would chicken out of racing down his hill on my bike if I saw any cars coming. I'm quite sure that a lot of the professionals and stars in my neighborhood would go running to their windows as they heard my screams as I chased my imaginary bad guys. Many of them, I'm sure had the displeasure of slamming on their brakes, and spilling their groceries, to avoid hitting me and my bike as I ran the stop signs. Ron Glass lived on my street, just a few houses down and I left a lot of blood on the sidewalk in front of his home. Skinned knees and elbows, as I tried to set the land speed record on my bike.

Someone from the music group, The 5th Dimension, lived so close to me; I wondered if they could hear my screams as my mother brutalized me. I'm sure that all of these celebrities that had dogs were a little disappointed at their behavior, when I would ride by. These fine, expensive, well trained, full pedigree, dogs would come unglued as I screamed by their homes and would bark and give chase to catch me on my bike. The Turners had a huge, Great Dane called "Onyx," and when he got loose, he would chase any child with legs. He especially loved to chase me on my bike and I would be so excited to give him a good run for his long legs. I always worried about what he would do to me if he ever caught me. He never did. I was too scared and peddled like my life depended on it. It would be the talk of the street amongst the children when Onyx got out. We all loved it!!

About seven or eight houses up the street lived Ike and Tina Turner. They have four boys about my age and younger. Ike Jr. was my age, then came Craig, Michael, and little Ronnie. We would play together whenever I was allowed outside. Christmas was awesome at the Turner house—four bikes, four electric guitars, four of everything so that there was always enough for us to get into.

They had the most awesome fish tank that was built into a wall so it could be seen from two rooms. It was huge with lots of fish. I've never seen anything like it. The boys were raised mostly by their maid, more so than I was. Only a couple of hours a day for me; but it could be days or weeks for them. I was too young to know what Ike Sr. and Tina were doing when they were on the road, but we kids had a lot of fun while they were gone.

I went there to play with the boys one day, and Mrs. Turner opened the door. She said the boys were gone. "Are you the little boy from down the street?" she asked. I said yes and she invited me in. That's when I saw her eye. It was really hurt because it was black and bloody. I started to cry and said to her, "Someone hurt you!" Then she started to cry and asked me why I was crying. I pulled up my shirt and showed her my bloody back and said, "Someone just hurt me, too."

We hugged each other and she took me to the piano bench and sat me down. She sat beside me and asked me if I liked music. I shrugged my shoulders and just kept crying as she sang us a song. I don't remember what song she played, but it was beautiful and soothing to the soul.

I have never forgotten that day. I always wonder if she remembers me. Why do people have to hurt other people? She was a nice lady, and I knew she didn't deserve what had happened to her. After she finished playing, we just sat there in silence. Finally, she got up and said, "You'd better be going." I left and never saw her again.

CHAPTER 7: SHE TRIED TO KILL ME WITH A CHAIR

Around my 11th birthday (and I never had birthday parties), I was expelled from Audubon Junior High and John Muir for fighting. Being light skinned at an all-black school, kids always wanted to beat me up. They called me a white boy and said things like "Kill the white boy" or "We're gonna get you, whitey!" I would tell them I'm not white, but that wouldn't do any good so, every day, I had at least one fight, some days two or three. Getting expelled, truthfully, probably saved my life, or theirs. Being hated by my mother was one thing. Now being hated by my own people, my own race, now this was really something else. I used to wonder if there was a sign on my back of some kind or a bulls-eye target located on my forehead, that read: hate me, kill me, beat me up, I enjoy it.

I was called, half-breed, high yellow, a wannabe, an Uncle Tom, an Oreo, a white boy, all sorts of horrible names. And it was mostly black people that called me these names. White people would call me half-breed, mutt, and other such horrible names also. So let me see if I got this thing right. I'm too dark to be white, so they hate me. I'm too light to be black, so they hate me also. My mother really hates me. So where do I fit in? It seems that everybody hated me for some reason or another.

Hey!! I did not fill out an application before I got to earth!! I did not get to choose what color I wanted to be! I did not get to choose my height, my weight, or how fast I can run. If we were all made by God, in His image, why do you hate me? I didn't even ask to be born, and was really starting to question why.

You know, if I was not fighting these black kids, I was running. If it were only one, or two, or even three kids, they would have a fight on their hands. This was why I was sent to the Principal's office every day I showed up for school. Oh yeah! I also knew when to run! But even running, I had a few tricks up my sleeves. Most mornings, I would have to hide behind the bungalows until the first bell, to avoid a fight. One particular morning, I was spotted by a group, as I got out of my mother's car. It was "on" immediately. I was a fast little guy, and as they chased, their line of warriors started to thin as I outran them. The fastest kid chasing me, I slowed down for, and turned around on him, and bloodied his nose. Then I noticed, the rest of them were not too excited anymore to catch me. Day after day, fight after fight, I really started to learn to hate them back. By the time they were done with me, I hated black people more than white people! Wow! What am I saying? My own people? Yeah! They hated me first!!

A few days later, I was playing in the driveway when Mom pulled up in her '57 Chevy Bel-Air—the one with tail fins with chrome tips on them. As she pulled in, one of the tips fell to the ground with a clang. I just stood there. She got out of her car and screamed, "What was that??!!"

I pointed and said, "It fell off as you pulled in the driveway."

She looked at it there on the ground and said, "What have you done to my car? Pick it up and put it back, right now!!"

So I picked it up and tried to put it back on the car, but it didn't stay. Much to my dismay, it fell to the ground again with a resounding clang. As it hit the ground, my heart just stopped, and I knew I was about to breathe my last breath. She *loved* this car way, way more than she even *liked* me. I was a goner for sure.

She stomped her foot and asked me what I had done to her car. I tried to explain that I had done nothing but stand there and watched her pull into the driveway when the piece just fell off. She told me I had two choices: if I continued to say that I had done nothing to her car, she would beat me for fifteen minutes with the razor strop; but, if I admitted that I had broken her car, she would beat me for only five.

Either way, I knew that this would be the worst beating of my life. I also knew from the look in her eyes that she would probably kill me this very day.

I started crying and again told her that it wasn't my fault and that it had just fallen off, and that I was nowhere near the car when it fell off. She knew I was nowhere near the car, and the car was moving when the piece came off, but she insisted that I had broken her car.

Believe me, if I could just look at something and it would be destroyed, I sure wouldn't have been looking at the tail end of her car! If looks could kill....

She screamed for me to go in the house to my room and take off all my clothes and wait until she got there. This was the first time I ever hit my knees and prayed. I said, "If there really is a God, you have *got* to kill her before she kills me. Would you please hit her with a lightning bolt or something?"

I really didn't know God and doubted that He knew me. Where was He really? How far was heaven from where I was about to have the snot beat out of me? Does He feel the same way about me as Mom does? Does He really love me? I thought, "He was supposed to protect us from harm. Could

44

He not see what was happening in my life? Aren't children included in the promises? God! Can you hear me?"

I could hear her coming up the stairs. I looked to where I thought Heaven should be and said, "*Now* would be a good time, Lord! *Please!!* Here she comes! *Save me!!*"

As I waited, I knew in my heart I had done nothing wrong. I didn't know how long fifteen minutes was, but it sounded a lot longer than five minutes. That was when she walked in and screamed, "I hate you! You little bastard!! Now tell me! What did you do to my car?!"

I said, "Nothing! I didn't do anything to your car!"

She beat me everywhere with that razor strop—legs, arms, buttocks, back, sides, and even hit me in the face. The louder I screamed, the more she got into it. She was swinging that strop with everything she had. There was no restraint. She was giving this all she could.

After what seemed like forever, the razor strop suddenly flew from her hand and went somewhere in the room where she couldn't find it. Nothing like that had ever happened before!

In her rage, she grabbed the oak chair in front of my desk

and hit me in the back with it, sending me crashing to the floor. She hit me with everything she had and I knew she was not going to stop this time. I could see it in her eyes. She was enjoying this too much.

When I hit the floor, all I saw was her ankle. I immediately grabbed it with all my strength, yanked it, and down she went like a fallen tree. With that, I grabbed up my discarded clothes and shoes and ran down the stairs, buck naked, out the front door to hide in the neighbor's bushes while I got dressed.

I was crying and bleeding with every part of my body hurt and stinging. As I dressed as quickly as I could, my heart raced as if it were about to explode in my little chest. I had just sealed my fate. If she caught me, I'd be one dead kid!

Suddenly, she ran out of the house with that razor strop, screaming at the top of her lungs! She wasn't screaming any words, just a blood curdling scream.

I stopped moving. I even held my breath as I became one with that bush. I still had to put on my shirt and shoes, but I didn't dare move or even breathe. My arms, back, and legs were bleeding and stinging like crazy, but I held my breath and gritted my teeth in pain. I watched as some blood was dripping silently down my arm, across my wrist, along my hand and then down one finger and began to drip, one drop at a time, plop, plop, plop, onto the leaves and dirt on the ground.

She looked up and down the street, then got into her car and drove really slow right past the bush where I hid. As she made a right at the corner, I finally took a deep breath, then quickly put on my shirt and shoes.

My heart kept racing in my chest as I tried to think about what I was going to do next. Which way should I run? Where could I go?

No mistake here, or she would catch me.

CHAPTER 8: RUNAWAY RABBIT

I knew I couldn't go back to that house ever again. I also knew that anywhere else on planet earth would be better than being there. I had a whole world out here to hide in. Although I was terrified and needed to run, my legs were so bloody and painful that they didn't want to move. I thought, "Hey! They worked well enough to get me away from sure death. They will have to work to get me out of here!"

I was about to bolt from the bush like a scared little rabbit when I saw her car coming slowly up the street. I held my breath and waited until she cruised by. She was searching around the trash cans and bushes, but she went right on by and on up the street, never even looking in my direction.

I bolted for freedom just as fast as my little legs could carry me, and I ran like the wind past two or three houses before leaping over and behind a huge hedge. I crawled up into a bush then looked up the street to see her turning the car around, so I bolted around the corner and into another bush where I waited to see if she had spotted me.

She slowly came down the street. I couldn't see the car, but I heard it. My heart pounded so hard I thought someone might hear it. Every nerve in my body was alive and screamed in pain.

49

Blood dripped down my arm. I didn't care, though. All I knew was that I was *not* going to be caught!

To my dismay, she turned the corner onto the street where I hid. I prayed, "Please, don't see me!"

I didn't dare breathe or move even a leaf on the bush where I hid. As she drove slowly past my hiding spot, I could see her frantically looking around, trying to find me. She drove on down the street and down the hill.

That was when I bolted back toward the house, all the while thinking, "Where is my sheriff friend? That's it!! I'll find him and tell him everything she has ever done to me. He *has* to help me!"

I ran like my life depended on it and didn't stop for about eight blocks. When I finally got to his famous stop sign, he wasn't there!! Oh, boy!! What now? Where is he?

I thought of another stop sign where he might be hiding, so I ran all the way there, about six or seven blocks away. I got there completely out of breath to discover he wasn't there either!

I thought of the spot where the Highway Patrol always sat, waiting to catch someone running the light. No longer able to run, I walked the two miles to Overhill and La Brea. Once again, no one was there. I just couldn't believe it!!

Out of breath, tired, and sore, I plopped down on the ground and just cried. Where was he? Why wasn't he here? I didn't have anywhere to go, but I knew I wasn't going back home.

Then I remembered what the coach said, "They have laws against this type of stuff." So I thought, "I'll go to the Southwest Police Station on Santa Barbara Boulevard. That's the only way out of this. I have to tell someone! Once I tell someone, everything will be just fine."

I walked and ran to the Police Station, probably six to eight miles away. I arrived a sweaty, bloody mess. I told the officer at the desk all that my mom had been doing to me. I just knew he would be able to help me somehow. That was when he said, "Go back home before you get another spanking."

That was it. Wow! I was shocked!

"You mean I came all this way and you are going to send me back home?"

I didn't know what else to do. I knew only that I couldn't go home, so I figured I'd better tell my dad that I was running away.

CHAPTER 9: DEAR DADDY

I walked back a couple of miles toward the Crenshaw Shopping Center to the Sav-on Drugs Store. I had seven cents to my name. I bought a pencil for four cents and went back down the aisle to sharpen it for free. Outside in the parking lot, I found a big piece of a brown paper bag and sat down on the curb to write my "goodbye, Dad" letter.

I wrote down all the things Mom had done to me, and then wrote down what had happened today. I told him about the look in her eyes. I told him that she would kill me for sure for telling him. I told him that I loved him and my brother and sister, but I couldn't go back home. I told him how I had escaped. I told him that I was running away.

I signed it with tears, then folded it up and walked across the street to the Crenshaw Medical Arts Center on Santa Rosalia Drive.

As I walked, I tried to figure out how to deliver this letter and still be able to get away. My problem was the elevator. His office was about 15-20 feet away from the elevator. When the doors opened, I planned to run as fast as I could to his office, slide the letter under his door where the nurses were, and somehow get back to the elevator before the doors closed.

I entered the lobby of his building. My heart pounded. As I waited for the elevator, I let my legs know that they had to move like never before.

Ding! The doors opened. I entered the elevator and pushed the button for the third floor. I had the pounding in my chest, and my throat was all choked up as tears started to roll down my cheeks. Up I went, praying that I would be fast enough to return back to the elevator so I could escape as planned. I was a mess, all covered with sweat and trickles of dried blood; my clothes were filthy from the dirt and the bushes. Luckily, I had the elevator all to myself.

Ding! The doors opened again and I bolted out of there as fast as I could. I ran to Dad's office door and skidded to a stop to quickly slip the note under the door before tearing back toward the elevator. With a super quick right turn, I got back to the elevator—just in time to see the doors closing! I slammed the elevator button, believing I had made it back just in time to make them open again—but they didn't.

My heart dropped and landed on the floor. I hit the elevator doors with my fists and felt a hand on my shoulder. Someone said, "Oh, no you don't! Come on back here with me."

It was Eva, my dad's head nurse. To me, she was like a mother ought to be: always so nice and sweet. I loved her a lot and even asked her once or twice why she couldn't be our mother.

I begged her to let me go, but she had a tight grip on my arm. As she led me back to my dad's office, I pleaded with her, "Please don't take me in! I *must* get away. She's going to kill me! You *have* to let me go!"

She looked me in the eyes as she told me, "Don't worry, child. Everything will be just fine. Your dad is in, and he'll want to see you."

As she opened the door, there was my dad, standing there wearing his white doctor's coat and stethoscope, reading my note. As he read, he looked at me. When we walked into his office, I ran into his arms and let loose the panic inside me.

"Please let me go! I can't go back home! She will *kill* me now that I have told you!"

I thought for a second that perhaps he didn't believe Mom could have done all the things I had written in the letter. He bent down to me, removed my shirt, and turned me around to look at my back. In disbelief, he examined me: fresh bloody wounds on top of old wounds; new blood on top of scabs now bleeding again; red hot welts raised in my flesh.

"I love you" was all I could whisper for a second. Then I managed, "Please, don't take me back home...."

Both of his nurses, looking at my back, had their hands over their mouths. Tears welled up in their eyes. I remember a tear or two in Dad's eyes, too.

He took me to his inner office and closed the door. He asked me to tell him everything.

I told him everything she'd ever done or said to me since she knocked me out of the high chair. He just shook his head and looked at me and said, "Why did you wait all these years to tell me?"

"She would have *killed* me! I just know she would have!"

He said he wished I had told him when it first started. Then he called in Eva to dress my wounds as best as she could. Once that was finished, he said, "Let's go."

"Lets go? Where?" I asked. As we got to the door, he told his nurses to hold his patients right where they were; that he'd be right back. I couldn't believe he would leave his office. He'd never done that before, so I asked him again, "Where are we going?"

As we walked to the elevator, he told me he was going to take me home. My heart dropped so far down that I think it landed in the lobby while we were still on the third floor waiting for the elevator. Hadn't he heard what I said? How could he take me home now after all he'd seen and heard?

I turned to run, but he had a hold of me before my feet got me going. "Where do you think you're going?"

"Dad, she'll *kill* me! You *can't* take me back!" He smiled and said, "Don't worry. She'll never touch you again."

I started crying again and told him, "You don't *know* her! As soon as you leave again, she'll *get* me! *Please*, Dad, I don't *want* to go home!"

"Where do you want to go, then?" he asked.

"*Anywhere!*" I said, "*Anywhere USA!* Let's leave here and get a house where she doesn't know where I am!!"

He smiled again as we got into the car. "We already *have* a house, and that's where we're going. Don't say anything to her and don't go *near* her. When we get home, just go to your room and don't come out. When I get home, I'll bring dinner. Just stay in your room. She will never hurt you ever again, do you hear me?"

"Yes, Dad, but I'm really scared. I wish there were some other way."

He told me there was no other way. I was sick. I was hurt. I was tired. I wanted to just disappear. I had run so very far to get away from home, and now we were on our way back home.

We approached the house with my little 11-year-old heart breaking apart in my chest. As we made our way into the front door, I was so scared that I grabbed Dad's hand and walked behind him to make him my shield as we entered the house. We went in to find her standing right there, just inside the door.

He shushed her when she started to ask what I was doing with him. I stood behind him, still holding his hand for dear life, but he pulled me around to face him, and sternly ordered, "Go up to your room and don't come out!"

I ran upstairs to my room and plopped down on the floor with my ear to the vent near the bottom of the wall. I heard some of what Dad said, "I don't care what he does or what he says! You will *not* touch him ever again! I saw what you did to his back! I know what you have been doing to him! This mustn't ever, *ever* happen again! Don't you know the trouble…?" I could just barely make out what he said after that, but he continued, "Then don't talk to him, I don't care. Don't you *ever* even think of touching him again. Never! *Never! Do you hear what I'm saying?*"

I heard his footsteps coming up the stairs, so I jumped up to go sit at my desk.

He told me not to be afraid, to take a shower, and to stay in my room until he got home when we'd eat dinner together. I begged him not to leave, but he assured me that I would be alright.

From that moment on, she never said a word to me, and from the next day on, my dad kept me with him all day, every day.

I loved it, being with him.

.

CHAPTER 10: YOUNG DOCTOR WIGGINS

My dad took me with him, and I loved it. In the mornings, we would go to different hospitals where he would perform surgeries, visit his patients, and whatever else doctors do. I would usually wait in the car and read. I didn't mind because I was away from Mom and with him. Then he would leave me at his office where his nurse Eva would take care of me.

I loved all the neat stuff my dad had in his office - all the gadgets and doctor stuff. If it moved or lit up, I would take it apart and put it back together again. I would read books and listen to country music. Country music was like music from Heaven to me. And I couldn't help crying when I heard Tammy Wynette or Loretta Lynn sing their songs. I thought they sang like angels. Their heavenly voices pierced my very soul. Had they been singing the Gospel, I would have gotten saved, healed, and delivered!

Being black and loving country music didn't seem to go over well back then. I listened to KLAC with an earpiece because you weren't supposed to listen to, or like, country music. You were expected to listen to soul music as it was called, or rhythm and blues, or at least the top forty. Not only did I listen to KLAC, but, I called in to make requests, then listened for hours to hear my requests.

Things my dad had in his office fascinated me. I would marvel at the x-ray machine and all the lights and power that went along with it. One time, I took apart the device he had to look into patients' ears and noses. It had a light, a magnifying glass, a cone to direct the light, and it was battery-operated. I took it apart to use the light bulb and batteries to light up my toy cars. That's when he walked in to see his instrument in pieces.

"What have you taken apart now? That's not a toy, you know, and it's very expensive."

"But, Dad, I can put it back together."

"Okay. Let's see."

I'd have it back together in seconds, then he would really scrutinize my work, pushing this and looking at that, until he was satisfied that it was as good as he had left it.

Then he'd say, "Good. Now don't take it apart again."

One day, I took apart his old antique office radio and soon had a million parts sitting on his desk. I had on my earphone listening to it when he walked in and said, "What's this?"

"Listen Dad, it works," I said so proudly as I held out the

earpiece to him.

He said, "That's an old antique radio. Will it go back together exactly like it came apart?"

"Of course," I said, "but, first, listen. It works!"

"Of course, it works," he said. "It worked before you took it apart. Please put it back together as it was."

"Okay, Dad, but it didn't have an earphone before, and now it does."

"It's not *supposed* to have an earphone, son. It's supposed to be heard all over the room."

"But, Dad," I insisted, just knowing that I'd invented something marvelous and great, "now I can listen without disturbing you when you work."

"Great," he said. "Now please, put it back together. And there are an awful lot of parts here you aren't even using. Are you *sure* you can put this back together?"

I smiled and said, "Of course I can, Dad. You just watch me!"

So I went to work and shortly thereafter, his radio was

back to its original form.

I did have one failure with a clock he had that swung these three balls down below its face. It had a glass dome and, although I got it all back together, it never worked again. Ooopps!! After that, he bought me electronic kits and models to work on. Because I think he was so amazed that I could put his radio back together, he bought me my own radio along with a soldering iron and solder and an electronic set to make my own radio from scratch.

It was on! My favorite store became Radio Shack, where I would buy lights, motors, wiring, switches, and all sorts of neat stuff to light my models and give them power.

I loved being with him and I loved his office. I told him I wanted to be just like him—a doctor. That didn't last long, however, after one of his patients came in the office after being hit by a car in front of his office building, and collapsed on the floor in the waiting room. How she walked into his office from the street, I didn't know.

My job at the time was to call the next patient and direct them to an examination room, so I was standing there when she fell, with blood and guts oozing out of her head. I went into shock and couldn't move or speak. Nurse Eva called my dad who started to work on her right away, right in front of me. Then the nurse picked me up and took me into his office and closed the door. I just stood there for hours it seemed, in shock from what I had seen.

Finally he came in and saw me still standing there. I started to cry. He sat with me at his desk and asked if I was all right. I told him no, and asked what was wrong with her. He explained that the car accident had cracked open her skull. He explained what he had done to save her. He assured me that she would live and was going to be just fine.

"This is what I do for a living; and if you want to be like me, you are going to have to get used to seeing things like this and not let it bother you. You'll have to get used to seeing blood."

I told him, "Dad, I don't want to be this kind of doctor."

He laughed and said, "You cannot be a doctor unless you can go inside of someone's body to fix and repair things."

I told my dad I didn't like the sight of blood and that there must be another kind of doctor I can become that doesn't go inside a person's body. "Outside only" was what I was thinking. He told me very plainly and simply, "If you cannot stand the sight of blood, you will never be a doctor."

I knew then, that I couldn't follow in his footsteps. It broke my heart because I wanted to be just like him. He was so cool, so calm, and so awesomely good at what he did. A top surgeon. Chief of surgery at different hospitals. Highly acclaimed in the medical profession. He is even in *Who's Who in America*. What skill he possessed! What devotion he had! In my eyes, he was the King of Surgery! But he said I must overcome my fear of blood and guts. That just wasn't in me.

Other doctors he knew would ask me, "Do you still want to be a doctor?" I would nod my head yes, before remembering that lady on my dad's waiting room floor. Then I'd shrug my shoulders and shake my head no.

My dad sometimes answered for me, "He wants to be a doctor, but he can't handle the blood." They would smile and say, "You'll get over it. Give it time."

I never did get over it.

CHAPTER 11: TRICKED AND LIED TO

One evening about three months later, Mom came to the door of my bedroom to ask me if I wanted to go to a place with a lot of boys my age, where we would play and have fun, and nobody would bother us. She said it was big and nice and had lots of room to play football and baseball. I was making a lanyard key chain at that time, and I asked her, "Can I sell my key chains there?"

She smiled as she answered, "I'm sure you can, they'd love your key chains. Do you think you'd like to go? It's like a summer camp and I think you would really like it."

I answered, "I guess so, it sounds nice."

She said, "Tomorrow we're going to see a man who can get you in. He may ask you a couple of questions. Just answer yes to whatever he asks you. He is going to ask you if you are incorrigible, and you just say yes. That means that you really want to go. Do you understand?"

"Yes" I said. "Just say yes."

"Good," she said.

She went back downstairs as I sat there trying to imagine

this beautiful place she described. I was so excited that I would be away from her, hopefully, really far; and that maybe my dad, brother, and sister would come to visit me there. I pictured huge grass fields with kites flying and kids riding bikes and playing catch. It was too perfect! Boy, I can't wait until tomorrow!

When we went to court—surprise, surprise! My mom never said we would be in a courtroom in front of a judge; she'd said "a man." The judge asked me, being 11 years old, if I understood what was going on. I looked at Mom. She gave me such a look that I went on and said, "Yes, Sir."

"Do you agree that you are incorrigible?" the judge asked, and I answered, "Yes Sir," since Mom had told me what that meant.

He asked me to leave the room. My mom and the attorney stayed for a few minutes.

When she came out, she said that I'd done very well and I would be able to go to this wonderland for boys tomorrow. We went home and I told my brother the good news and all that I had imagined about this incredible place I would be going to.

The next day, Mom and Dad and I left the house to take me to this wonderful place for growing boys like me. I was so excited and so relieved that it was really true, that I would be leaving. I wanted to be as far away from her as I could get, and this was my dream come true, a kid's dreamland, filled with cotton candy, licorice whips, and baseball—all day long!

CHAPTER 12: WHERE ARE WE GOING...REALLY?

We drove what seemed like hours, and then pulled up in the place, a huge place with lots of buildings, lots and lots of grass, and lots of trees. The grass looked beautiful to play on, and the trees looked fun to climb, but the buildings looked old and gray and scary.

Where were the kids? There was no one outside playing. Part of me was elated, the other part, apprehensive.

"What's wrong with the buildings?" I asked.

"Nothing is wrong. That's where the children are," Mom answered.

As we got closer and parked, my heart raced. I was anxious to get away from her, but something didn't seem right about these buildings. They were cold and gray and looked uninviting to me.

I asked, "Are you sure we're at the right place?"

My dad got out with me and brought a suitcase. I didn't remember packing anything. My mom sat in the car as my dad and I went up some stairs. As I looked, I could see something was wrong with the windows of these ugly buildings. As we reached the top of the stairs, I could see bars on the windows.

That's what was wrong! The glass of the windowpanes had wire screen inside, and the windows had bars on the inside and outside of them. I felt that, once inside, I would never be able to get out. The sign on the door read:

Camarillo State Hospital

Mental Ward

I told my dad we were in the wrong place. He pushed the button at the door. The door buzzed and my dad pulled the door open. I went in first.

About four or five feet from the door we just came through was another door with a glass window in the middle of it. Just like the windows I had seen in the rest of the building, there was wire inside the glass in these doors. I stood on my tippy toes to look in and saw a long hallway with lots of people in it: children and adults. None of them were acting normal. Some were standing, others were walking back and forth. Several of them were drooling saliva from their mouths. A lot of them were deformed. Some were screaming. Some were making weird noises.

I turned around to my dad and said, "We are *definitely* in the wrong place!"

He was still holding the outside door open when we heard a voice over the speaker telling us that the outer door must be closed to open the inner door. My dad was trying to manipulate the luggage, the outside door, and me while I was trying my hardest to get out of the outside door! I had one leg out and both hands on the door to keep it from closing, and he was trying to pull it closed, telling me to let go.

Tears filled my eyes, and my heart was tearing in my chest. I couldn't believe for one minute that this was the place Mom had found for me. There had to have been a mistake!

"Daddy, please don't leave me here! Can't you see there's crazy people in there and I'm not crazy! Daddy, please! This is a mistake. Mommy said it would be a wonderful place for boys my age. We're at the wrong place. Please don't do this to me. I'm not crazy!"

I was holding onto the door for dear life and my dad couldn't pry me off. I was crying and my chest was burning as I screamed, "Please Daddy, don't leave me in this place!"

The speaker spoke again saying that security was on the way. Soon, three guys in white smocks were on the other side of the inner door. A buzzer sounded and the inner door opened setting off an alarm. They grabbed me and pulled me inside, screaming and kicking.

"Daddy, Daddy, please help me! Don't let them take me!"

He had tears in his eyes as he followed us through the inner door.

I got away from them and grabbed my dad's leg and pleaded with him, "Please don't leave me here, I'll be good. I love you Daddy! Don't do this! Take me somewhere else, please! I'm not crazy!!"

He looked down at me with tears in his eyes and said, "There's nothing I can do. You'll be all right."

And then one of the men in white coats held me. My dad pulled away from my grasp and quickly walked away. He passed through the doors and the alarm went quiet as both doors closed behind him.

I watched him disappear, one step at a time, down the stairs, and all hope left with him. My heart shattered in my chest. I couldn't believe that my dad, the dad I loved so much, could leave me in a place like this. He was crying, too, so he had to have felt that this was wrong.

"Don't leave me," I murmured.

"Please don't leave me here."

CHAPTER 13: I'M NOT CRAZY!

I was on my knees facing the two doors. Eleven years old with no hope, no love, no one to love, broken hearted, crying like a baby, scared to be abandoned in the Camarillo State Hospital mental ward. I felt unwanted and thrown away. My shirt was so wet with tears that I started to shiver. I was so cold, and I was now a prisoner in this evil place which was supposed to be my wonderful new home. What am I supposed to do now? I loved my dad so much, but all of his strength and protection had just walked out of my little life and left me in a place I couldn't possibly begin to understand.

I had been left to fend for myself in a place mixed with children and young adults, a place where society hid away those they didn't want to see, those who brought them shame. Some had physical and mental disabilities, birth defects, or were otherwise physically deformed. Others were criminally insane or child molesters. How could anyone do this to a beloved child? Did my parents really believe I was crazy?

All that I loved had been taken from me at the age of eleven. I had been separated from my dad, brother, and sister, and was branded as insane. I knew Mom had lied about everything, and I imagined the satisfaction she must have felt in knowing that if this place didn't kill me, it would drive me out of my mind, and then I would become a permanent resident. As good as dead!! With all of that, I felt even more just how *much* Mom hated me. My hatred for her rose to a new, horrific level.

At that time, I didn't know how I could survive; but, in my little broken and torn heart, I knew I would. I had to get out some way, some how. I planned to torture Mom slowly before killing her. For every day I had to spend in this horrible place, I would repay her the same amount of days, torturing her. Then I would kill her!! I really, really, *really* hated her —with a passion!

How can I escape? Where would I go? A hand gently touched my shoulder and a soft voice asked me if I was all right. I turned around to see Clark. A tall, muscled, tanned, and brown-haired man. He looked at me with kind eyes.

In my tears, I begged, "Please help me! I'm not crazy! I don't belong here, and I'm scared."

He knelt down on one knee and said, "Come here, little boy."

He hugged me and said, "You'll be alright, don't worry."

I had never been hugged before, but I felt safe in his arms

and I asked him if he was a daddy. He smiled and wiped my tears with the back of his big strong hand and said, "Yes, I have two boys about your age."

With tears still flowing, I asked, "Would you ever leave them in a place like this?"

His smile left as he looked into my tear-filled eyes. He looked as if he were searching inside me, looking and searching me through and through. Then he softly said, "Never!"

He was still holding me and I shook his hands away from my shoulders so I could take off my shirt. I turned around to show him the scars on my back, healed but still evident. They looked like stripes. I asked him, "Would you ever do this to your boys?"

He turned me around and put my shirt back on me, then hugged me again. He looked into my eyes with those piercing eyes of his and wiped my tears as he asked, "When did this happen? And who did this to you?"

He looked like he was going to cry with me, but he held it back. I told him that Mom did it, and that I don't know why she hates me. I added that it had happened a few weeks ago, but was always happening as far back as I could remember. He asked me what my first memory was. I told him about being knocked down while in my high chair when I was two years old.

He hugged me again and said, "C'mon, we have to get up and out of this hallway." I started crying again and told him I didn't want to go into this place. I said that I didn't belong here, there's been a mistake because I'm not crazy, and there was nothing wrong with me. He picked up my luggage and held my hand and said, "I believe you, Kiddo. I know you're not crazy, and I'm going to help you, but I can't help you sitting here in the hallway. You have to come to my office."

A lot of people were in the hallway. Most were really insane, just rocking back and forth, so I told him that I was really scared. I pointed at the others and said I wasn't like that.

"Just hold my hand and follow me," he said. "I won't let anything happen to you. Just don't look at anyone and everything will be alright."

As we started down the hall, a kid who was as tall and as big as a man started screaming and yelling and fighting a man in a white coat. Clark pushed me against the wall and told me not to move.

He picked up the crazy man from behind and pinned his arms to his sides before taking him to a room with a sign that read "Shock Treatment."

Children ran to the door of the room to listen; and about five to seven of them came over to me and started touching me. I just froze and closed my eyes and stood there, scared to death of this place. It seemed like forever as they touched my hair and face and arms. I just kept my eyes closed and stood there, afraid to move. I was crying, but not because they were hurting me. It was because I was so scared. They kept touching me, and I didn't understand why. I wanted them to go away and leave me alone, and I wished that Clark would come back.

To make things worse, I heard terrible screams coming out of the room. Clark finally came out and gently removed the children who were touching me. He knelt down beside me, looked me in the eyes, and said, "I'm sorry about this. Are you alright?"

I leapt into his arms, crying, and asked, "What were they doing to me? Why were they touching me?"

He explained that they weren't trying to hurt me. "They're special," he said, "and were just trying to say hello, not to hurt you. That's just how they act when they meet someone they don't know. And some of them are blind, so they 'see' with their hands."

He pulled my hand down from my eyes and took my hand and led me on down the hallway. As we passed the room with the sign that said "Shock Treatment," I asked what happened to that man he took in there. Clark explained that this man was what they called a "psycho" and that he loved to attack little boys. He said that when the man got out of control, he would be strapped down to a table and shocked with electricity to calm him down.

Clark opened the door and showed me. The psycho's name was Chris, and he was laying flat on a tall bed, with straps tying down his legs, arms, chest, and head. He had a stick in his mouth and wires attached to his head. His eyes, with black rings around them, looked as if they were sinking into his skull. As we gazed upon him, Chris was quiet, and I asked if he was still alive. Clark pointed out that Chris' chest was rising and falling. "Yes, he's alive; but he will sleep until tomorrow sometime because he was given a shot in his posterior. When he wakes up tomorrow, his rump will be so sore so he won't be able to sit down comfortably for a week."

Clark knelt in front of me and told me, "Kiddo, whatever you do, don't ever lose control or throw a tantrum in this place 'cause this is where you'll end up. Shock treatment causes you to lose your memory."

I thought, "Oh, no! They'll make me forget my dad and where I come from!"

Clark took me by the hand and led me to his office. I looked at the pictures of his family alongside pictures of helicopters. I asked him why the helicopters, and he said that he was going to fly them for the Sheriff's Department. He asked me some questions about my past and my family as he was writing.

I asked, "Clark, can you get me out of here?"

He looked at me with that look of his and said, "Kiddo, I'm sorry. Looks like you're stuck with me for a while...."

I cried and told him that this was a mistake, that I wasn't crazy. "So, how come Mom was able to put me here?"

He looked at some papers on his desk and said, "You told the judge that you were incorrigible."

Crying, I said, "My mom told me to say yes to everything. She said that word means that I wanted to go to this wonderful place where boys my age play and have fun."

Clark looked at me and asked, "Do you know what incorrigible means?"

Sobbing, I looked at him and said, "I guess not. What does it mean?"

Clark explained, "It means that you are out of control, that no one can control you. You didn't know?"

I was shocked and I looked at him, knowing now that Mom had tricked me and trapped me here. "I'm only eleven. I never heard that word!"

I asked Clark, "Isn't there a way I can get out of this place? Isn't there something I can do? Can I tell the judge what she did?"

He looked at me with those eyes of his. He chewed on the end of a pencil, deep in thought, then said that I wouldn't be able to see the judge because I was already here. What's done is done.

However....

My little heart leaped when I heard that "However." Clark continued, "...There is one thing we could do whereas the hospital would have to release you."

"Yes? Yes? Yes?" I was already out of my seat, and around the desk and almost into his arms as he explained that if the

Chief Psychiatrist was in today, I could take a battery of tests and, upon an examination of the scores of these tests, there *might* be a chance that the hospital would have to release me.

"Are you willing to take these tests?" he asked.

"Oh, yes! Please! Let me take those tests!" I nearly screamed.

Clark picked up his phone and made the call. "Hi, this is Clark. I'm bringing you a child, a new arrival, who I don't believe belongs here, and I would like you to test him. Yes, give him every test you have. Thank you. We will be right there."

Clark led me by the hand into the hall where all the other inmates were. He noticed how hard I squeezed his hand and told me to relax. "It's just down the hall."

We arrived at the Chief Psychiatrist's office and Clark introduced me to the Chief. His name was Bill. Bill was a short man with glasses who smiled as I came in. He sat me down at a desk and gave me a pencil and a pile of papers and told me to answer as many of the questions as I could. He also told me that I would be timed, so if I came to a question I couldn't answer, I would need to pass it by for the next one, and go back to it if I had extra time.

Bill asked me if I knew why I was here, but before I could answer, Clark took him outside the room and told me to start the test. Boy, were there ever a lot of questions, and I worked fiercely to answer them all quickly.

After a little while, Clark and Bill came back in. Clark asked me to show Bill my back. I turned around and raised my shirt. Bill put his hand up to his mouth, turned around, then quickly left the room. Clark told me to keep working, that lunchtime was just a few minutes away.

Clark ran after Bill as the door closed. I kept working, just knowing that I could pass this test because it was so simple. Just answer the questions. I kept writing until Clark and Bill returned and announced it was lunchtime.

I told them, "That's okay; I'm not hungry. I want to finish these tests."

Clark said, "Come on. The food really isn't that bad. Besides, I want to talk to you anyway."

So we walked hand in hand and got in line behind the other kids, most of whom were older than I was. Some seemed to be into their twenties; and some were giants compared to me. Most of these kids had physical deformities you could see; but some who looked "normal" couldn't talk or hear or see. Some looked alright, but were mentally challenged and could barely have a conversation.

When we reached the cafeteria and got our trays, we sat down right in the middle of a long table filled with kids. I tried to eat but couldn't. Looking around the room, I couldn't believe my eyes. Kids were smearing food all over their faces and the fronts of their shirts, and spitting up food down their chins and necks. Seeing this, I was about to be sick, so I told Clark. He grabbed his tray and said, "Let's get out of here. I'm sorry. I forgot how they eat. Pretty gross, huh?"

I swallowed carefully and squeaked, "Why do they eat like that?"

Clark explained that because of their mental incapacities and lack of hand-eye coordination they might miss more than they eat. I told him it made me sick to my stomach to watch them. Clark said, "Well, you can eat with me where the staff eats."

"Thank you," I said, "but I don't plan to be here that long."

He smiled and said, "Let's get back to your tests."

When I finished all of the written tests, Bill showed me

flashcards and ink spots and recorded my answers. When he finally said we were finished, he said I could lie down on his couch while he tabulated my score. I fell asleep for a little while. Clark woke me up with a big smile. His eyes were so excited as he looked into my sleepy eyes. I got up as he said, "Come here, Kiddo. We have some good news for you!"

He brought me back to Bill's desk and we sat down. With both of my hands, I held onto Clark's big hand and Bill said, "Eddie, this has never happened here before, but I want you to know that you passed every single test and I declare that, in my opinion, you are a healthy and mentally exceptional young lad. I have stated in this letter to your parents that it would be hazardous to your mental health to have you remain in our custody. You are hereby released by Camarillo State Hospital and you are free to be released to your parents or a legal guardian."

You cannot imagine how happy I was to hear this news! I hugged Clark so hard that he laughed. Then I ran around the desk and gave Bill the biggest hug I could. I thanked them both for believing in me, and giving me a chance to prove myself.

I knew in my heart I was about to be set free.

CHAPTER 14: THE NIGHTMARE BEGINS

Clark reached across the desk to pick up the phone. He asked me for my telephone number, which I quickly gave him. I sat in anticipation of the joy my dad would feel when he found out that I was released and free to come home. The words "Daddy come get me," rang in my little heart. Clark held the phone as it rang at my house.

"Please pick up the phone! Please answer! Please be there!"

Finally, Clark said, "Hello? Yes, ma'am. My name is Clark. I am the Head Technician and Counsellor at Camarillo State Hospital mental ward. I'm calling to let you know that it would be detrimental to Eddie's mental health to allow him to remain in our custody. I'm sorry, ma'am, but we have tested and evaluated your son and have found that he is mentally stable and not incorrigible. We have officially released him, so you will have to remove him immediately from our custody. I have his release papers in my hand as we speak. Yes, ma'am, I can do that."

There was a pause and I was thinking, "Oh, no. My mom picked up the phone."

"Clark," I implored, "ask for my dad!"

Clark asked my mom, "May I speak to Dr. Wiggins?"

I waited, hoping that she would give him the phone. "Please, Dad. Pick up the phone!" I thought.

"Then we will have to charge you for every day you leave him here with us."

All of a sudden, Clark put the phone back on the receiver. Tears filled my eyes as I asked, "What did she say? What happened?"

Clark reached down and picked me up in his arms. His look pierced through my tears and he hugged me.

"I'm sorry, Kiddo. She was so mad that I could feel her anger through the phone! She said she doesn't want you, that she could care less what we do with you, and then she hung up!"

My heartbreak was so intense that I knew Clark could feel my heart explode into little pieces in my chest as he held me. I cried uncontrollably, and he just held on, telling me that everything would be all right.

I thought I was doomed to remain here and that was too much for me to handle—a sane little boy locked up with criminals and the mentally ill. What would become of me? Would I become crazy, too? Would they try to kill me, too? What was it about me that made people hate me? Did everybody hate everybody? Did all mothers hate their children, or was it just mine? Was I all alone in this world of misery, or did I have company? Why me? Being so young, I couldn't begin to understand what was happening to me. I thought that you are born into this world, you have life, some have a good life, and some have a bad life. Some like me have a horrible life. But why me, what did I do?

Clark was so nice to me, yet he was so big and strong. To me, his name was like Clark Kent, a.k.a. Superman. With our failed attempt to have me released, I looked to him to be my Superman until I could rejoin my dad. I wiped my tears, looked into his eyes, and pleaded with him, "I don't know what's happening to me, and I'm so scared of this place. Will you make sure I don't go crazy in this place? Can you protect me and make sure nobody kills me in here?"

He squeezed me tightly and looked into my soul with those eyes, "Yeah, Kiddo. I will look after you until we can get you out of here. You can eat all your meals with me. You can work for me during the days, which will keep you busy and away from the other inmates. If you stay close, listen, and obey what

I tell you, you will be alright. I won't let anything happen to you. I promise. Okay?"

I trusted and believed in him and told him so. Then I thanked him. He also told me that I would have to sleep in a dorm with about ninety other "children" and that I would need a "friend." We left Bill's office with a big thank you and good-bye, and Bill promised that he would mail the release letter every week until it reached my dad.

CHAPTER 15: A LIGHT IN A VERY, VERY DARK PLACE

Clark led me down the hall to an almost empty dorm room with only a handful of children in their bunks, reading or sleeping. Clark showed me my bunk and locker. My luggage was already at the foot of my bed. Clark instructed me to start putting my things in the locker so he could put my empty suitcase in the storage locker. As I unpacked, he called a kid named Darrell Biggers to come over. He told me I would really like Darrell, that he wanted me to be Darrell's best friend.

Darrell walked with a limp and looked just a little weird. His parents were rich and had a lot of dinners and parties at their home so they put him here because they were ashamed to have a child who looked different. Darrell had an extra large head that was shaped like a football. He was a genius, though, and had a wonderful personality.

Darrell came over and Clark said, "Darrell, didn't I tell you I'd find you a really nice friend? Darrell, I want you to meet Eddie. Eddie, meet Darrell. I want you to be best friends. I want you to watch out for each other, help each other, and stay together at all times. Okay?"

Darrell had the biggest smile and stuck out his hand and

said, "Will you really be my friend?"

I shook his hand and said, "Yes, I need a friend. I really do."

His smile got even bigger as he hugged Clark and told him thank you.

Clark told Darrell to show me all the ropes of this place. He then told us that Darrell would be having dinner with us earlier than usual. Darrell grinned and said, "You mean, we get to eat with the staff?"

"Yes, Darrell," Clark replied with a smile. As he walked away, he added, "And all the ice cream you guys can eat."

"Yeah! All Right!" Darrell said. And then Darrell shook my hand again and said, "Don't worry, I know everything about this place and Clark won't let anything happen to you because he's been protecting me. Nobody messes with me because they know that Clark will kill them but good, and even if Clark's not around, they know I will tell him, and then Clark will kill them."

Darrell told me that his best friend had been transferred to another part of the hospital so he'd really felt alone, but Clark had promised him a new friend. He told me you can't talk to just anyone around here, and that it's better just to not talk to anyone else.

Darrel asked me why I was here, so I told him how my mom had tricked me and that she hated me. He said, "No big deal. My head's too big and I walk funny, but I'm not crazy either. My parents are ashamed of how I look, so they left me here 5 years ago. Sometimes they come and pick me up and I get to see my brother and sister. They look normal and we get along just fine. My brother and sister love me no matter what. It's my mom and dad. They don't want anyone to know that they have a kid with a deformed head. Got to keep appearances, you know…."

I told Darrell about my mom beating me and trying to kill me. I showed him my back. He said it looked like I had stripes and that with just a few stars I could be a flag. We both laughed.

Darrell told me his brother and sister were "normal" and he liked to play with them, but his parents prevented him from going outside to play because someone might see him. Instead, he was kept in his room because his parents were afraid of what their friends might think—they were ashamed of him.

I told him that I wasn't ashamed of him and that he was

the first kid I had ever shown my back to and told my story to. I told him that it was his smile that won me over immediately and that I would be proud to be his friend. He asked me if he could hug me. I said yes, so we hugged and shook hands again.

Darrell took me to his bunk and showed me all of his books. Darrell was a smart kid who read everything he could get his hands on. He was proud of his collection of books and told me briefly what some of them were about. When I asked him where he got them, he said that Clark always brought him new books. I told him that I really liked Clark and that Clark reminded me of Superman. He told me that Clark would be our only protection in this horrible place, and that no one would mess with us because of Clark.

Darrell loved Edgar Rice Burroughs and had every Tarzan book in the series, even the paperbacks. He gladly loaned me a few after I told him that I liked Tarzan and had read five or six of the paperbacks before arriving at this hospital.

Eddie at 9 or 10

"Let's go. I'll give you a tour," Darrell said.

When he told me about the 'time out shots,' he warned me

that any child or adult who displayed anger or got close to being out of control would be taken to the Shock Treatment room and given a shot that puts him to sleep for a day or two. After that, he wouldn't be able to sit down for about a week. This is what Clark had told me about Chris. I asked Darrell if he had ever had one. He said he never had, and didn't want one today either. We grinned at each other, and he took me to the door of the Shock Treatment room. He whispered, "Listen."

We put our ears to the door and could hear a sound from the machine and the screams from some poor kid. Darrell told me that you could tell which kids got the shock treatment because their eyes would sink deeper and deeper into their skulls and get black rings around them. He said most of them would drool and sit in a daze for about a week afterwards. He warned me to stay away from the "dark eyes." I asked again if they had ever done that to him and he said, "Never, but let me be first in line behind you!" Again, we grinned at each other and I said, "Thanks, but I think I'll pass."

CHAPTER 16: THE GANG

A group of small kids came over to us. It was the same group that I'd met in the hallway before when Clark had left me on the wall and told me not to move. The "touchy-feely" kids.

Darrell said, "Don't move, Eddie, they're okay. This is how they say hello."

These children touched our faces, hands, and arms. They touched Darrell and me, and Darrell introduced me to them. Although most of them couldn't see with their eyes, Darrell said they could see with their hands. He told me that they liked to touch only the "kind kids," the ones who wouldn't do them any harm. I asked him how they could tell who was nice and who wasn't. Smiling, he said, "Oh, don't you worry. They just know. Hah! They know!"

There were about seven kids in their group. Darrell explained that their leader could see, but couldn't talk or hear. He would lead the group around all day and they would gather around and touch only the nicest kids. He told me that they liked me, so I hugged each one of them and told them that I liked them, too.

Boy!!! They liked that! A couple of them squealed with joy and a couple jumped up and down in their excitement. Darrell had never seen them react like this, and he asked me, "What made you hug them?" I told him that they were probably unwanted and unloved like us. I added that I didn't know exactly what compelled me to give each one a hug, but they need love, too, and giving them a hug made them feel better, so it made me feel better, too.

Then Darrell gave each one of them a hug. Oh! They were so excited, and Darrell said, "You're right, Eddie! They liked it and I feel so good inside."

From then on, every day, three or four times a day, "the gang," as we started to call them, would find us and touch and hug us. "Here comes the gang," we'd say. "Get ready!"

Darrell was secretly showing me all the dangerous people in the dorm, mostly the older kids who were twenty and over; but there were a few dangerous types who were maybe fifteen and up. Darrell didn't dare point with his finger, so he would point like this: "Look straight ahead, but look at the kid leaning on the pole. See him? Okay, now look at the kid tying his shoe. He's one. Don't even look him in the eye. If he's coming toward you, go into an office and ask a question, or go the other way."

Darrell strongly advised that we stay on our bunks and be together at all times when Clark was not in sight. Stay to ourselves and we'd be alright. He told me that all the trouble and fights would occur in the TV room where most of the children hung out most of the time. The dorm was a safe spot since hardly anyone would be there except to sleep.

Bathrooms were never safe, especially during the night. We would go to the bathroom only as a team. Never alone. One to go, and the other to watch. For after lights out, Darrell gave me a plastic jar he called a piss pot. "Use it, dump it in the morning, and rinse it out. Keep it clean or it will smell. Put pennies in it during the day and keep it in the bottom of your locker. By day, it's a penny bank; at night, it's a lifesaver. People do weird things in the bathrooms, especially at night. If they see you in there, they'll try to do something weird to you." I asked Darrell what if you have to do a Number Two at night? "If you're smart, you'll put a cork in it and wait 'til morning."

Clark found us and said, "C'mon kids, let's eat." As we were walking by the other kids with Clark, someone pointed at me and said, "Hey, he's a new fish!" Clark said to the whole room in a huge, loud voice, "If you touch either one of my kids you'll go to the Shock Treatment room, and then I'll kill you. Do you understand? These two are off limits! They are mine!"

Not a whisper was heard in the room. "Wow!" I thought. "I really appreciated our Superman." And everyone else was scared to death of him.

As we were in line with our trays, Clark told the food servers to give us anything, and everything, we wanted. I was so hungry and this food looked great: burgers, pizza, sandwiches, chicken, and spaghetti. You name it; it was there: pies, cake, cookies, fruit, and ice cream! Wow! I'd never seen anything like it. And we could even have seconds. Clark was an eater like Darrell and I, so we all took our time. We all enjoyed it and, of course, we all had seconds on dinner as well as dessert.

I thought, "What an unbelievable day. As bad as it was, Clark and Darrell (and Bill) were so kind and gentle and great at dealing with a miserable situation." After dinner, Clark walked us back to our dorm and said he'd check in on us later. We thanked him as he left to feed the rest of the unit.

Darrell had a big smile on his face looking at me. "What?" I asked. "That was the best meal I've eaten here in five years, thanks to you and Clark." I looked bewildered and he said, "The rest of them are going to be eating S.O.S. for dinner. Most of the food we are fed is horrible. Because of you and what Clark's doing for you—letting us eat in the staff dining room and keeping me glued to you—I'm getting the good food, too. This is going to be great! Just great!" Darrell belched and giggled and repeated, "Just great!"

My first night was so scary! Clark made Darrell and me say our prayers before everyone went to bed and all the lights went out. I silently thanked God for Clark and Bill, and especially for Darrell. I had never had a best friend. What a terrible and horrible place this was, but I at least had a friend. It would be a lot worse without Clark and Darrell. A lot worse.

I thought about my dad and brother and especially my little sister. She was only two years old and had no idea what had happened with me. Would she even remember me when and if we ever saw each other again? Would she forget she had a big brother who loves her? What would my mother tell her about me? Would Mom turn her against me, too? What were they doing right now? Did they even know I was in danger?

I wanted to cry, but had no tears left. I was so tired. So lost. So scared. What would happen to me? Would I lose my mind in this crazy house? Would I become crazy, too? Is "crazy" something you can catch from other crazies like you can catch a cold?

I jumped up at the sound of a child screaming loudly.

During the night, I heard other children crying themselves to sleep. Another child screamed out, "I hate this place! I want to go home!"

I thought, "I know what you mean, kid. I know exactly what you mean." I fell asleep and had horrible dreams about where I was.

I awoke to a loud scream. "What was that?" I thought.

I got up and went across the aisle and down a couple of bunks to Darrell's bunk. As I approached, he sat up and asked, "Who is it?"

"It's me, Darrell, Eddie. I heard a loud scream. It woke me up."

"Probably some poor kid getting raped. Don't worry about it. Go back to sleep."

"Raped? What's that?" I asked him.

"Go back to sleep before they get you. You shouldn't be out of your bunk. I'll explain it to you in the morning. Look, man, you have to get tough in this place. You can't show your fear, especially in this place. They prey on the weak and the fearful. Get tough, Eddie, real quick. You get tough, okay?"

CHAPTER 17: GETTING TOUGH

From that night on Darrell and I stuck to each other like glue, watching out for each other, taking no chances, allowing for no mistakes. Clark had removed Darrell from the school and allowed him to work at his own pace, providing him with all kinds of work, but Darrell flew through each book and passed every test with an "A."

Darrell and I stuck together all morning and then again after lunch. Tokens were a requirement in this hellhole since breakfast was five tokens, and you had to use tokens for lunch and dinner, too. When you got up each day, you were required to make your bed, and keep the area between your bed and locker spotless. This would earn you seven tokens. You could also earn tokens by being good in class, cleaning up, and doing your homework.

I didn't go to the school with the rest of the kids. Clark had me on special detail: washing windows, sweeping, mopping, and waxing floors. Sometimes I would work in his office; other times, he would have school work for me to do.

He gave me lots of tokens for what I did so I earned about thirty tokens most days. For ten tokens, I could go outside where there was lots of grass and room to play and run. Clark gave Darrell and me balls and stuff to play with. I had to pay Darrell's way outside as well as mine, but I never minded that. He was my best and only friend, and he knew his way around this huge place really well.

Outside was also a payphone. Clark left dimes in a jar on his office desk and told me I could use them whenever I needed them since the payphones didn't take the tokens I was piling up, only real money. Clark knew that my main reason for going outside was to get to that payphone so I could call my dad at his office.

I called my dad's office at least twice a week. His nurse Eva answered most of the time and asked how I was, and if I was okay. Often, my dad wasn't there, but every once in a while, he was. On those rare occasions, I got to actually speak to him.

"Oh Daddy, I love you so much! Why won't you come get me? I want to come home. Please, Daddy, come and get me. Please don't leave me here!"

I pleaded with my dad to come for me, but he told me he hadn't received a letter stating that I had been released. I told him that Mom was probably tearing them up. He told me that a man named Bill had called his office, but he was not there to get the calls. I told him who Bill was and that he was trying to tell him that I had been released.

My dad was always too busy to talk for very long. It seemed to me that the longer we were physically apart, the more we grew farther apart as father and son. I wanted nothing more in the world than to come home, but my dad seemed powerless to do anything.

I wondered to myself what Mom had on him to make him do this to me. I couldn't believe that my being gone was okay with him. Didn't he miss me as much as I missed him? Didn't he want me to come home as much as I wanted to come home? What kind of power did Mom have over my dad to make him give me up? I would never give up. Somehow, someway, I would get back to be with my dad. I would never, ever give up.

One day Darrell took me to a building with a bowling alley in it. A nice man named Floyd ran the place. He was old, black, tall, and very thin. He liked us a lot so he would even let us bowl when we were short of tokens. He was very nice and always laughed and smiled a lot and smoked a pipe. He greeted us with a smile and then laughed and said, "Well, if it isn't two of the greatest bowlers in the whole wide world! Come on in, gentlemen! Let's throw some balls!" We always had a great time with Floyd.

On the outside, Darrell was always on his guard. He told me, "Watch this guy, Eddie. He's dangerous," and we went a different way to avoid trouble.

On the inside, Darrell was the smartest kid in the whole place. Even the counselors came to Darrell to ask questions. He was a genius of sorts. If he didn't know something, he'd find the answer in one of his books. One day as we walked around just talking, two of the child molesters got into a fight and were really trying to kill each other! We moved "the gang" out of harm's way as these two older boys tried their best to kill each other. By the time the counselors got them to stop fighting, they were a bloody mess. During their fighting, they had knocked a few of the really crazy people over, and one of the innocent bystanders was really hurt.

These two warriors were escorted straight to the Shock Treatment room.

Darrell told me, "Come on, let's listen!"

We put our ears to the door and listened as they screamed like we had never heard anyone scream before. Over and over, you could hear the switch and almost feel the power of the machine that poured out their punishment. It was so terrible to hear a person get the snot shocked out of them.

Most of the people who got shock treatment would wet and mess their pants. The black rings that formed around their eyes afterwards was scary to look at, making them look like zombies when they came out. The more times they went in, the farther back into their skulls their eyes seemed to go, and the blacker the rings became around their eyes.

Darrell explained to me that, if you went into this room enough, you would eventually become a "vegetable," because shock treatment literally fried your brains. I made sure I was always good and stayed away from anyone who even looked like trouble, which was mostly everyone except for Darrell, the "gang," and the really crazy lunatics. The really crazy ones would just sit and rock and drool all over themselves. Some of them would just walk the halls all day, and others would stand there in one place and rock standing up, drooling all over themselves; but they weren't dangerous to anyone.

I knew in my heart that I was not as bad off as a lot of these people. Most of them would never get out of this place. They would just rock and drool until they died, then they would finally be free of this horrid place.

And then there were the criminally insane: people who were extremely dangerous, who had done some of the most brutal crimes against society. The unspeakable, Darrell would say, are the ones to be watched, along with the child molesters. He really kept an eye on them. We both did. Every night was the same. Lights out, children crying themselves to sleep, screams during the night from nightmares and children getting raped. Screams that curdled your blood.

My hate for my mom raged on like an out-of-control forest fire. How could she do this to me? How could anyone do this to anyone? What is wrong with the people in this world?

CHAPTER 18: AN ANGEL IN A DARK PLACE

One day, Darrell told me that there was a dance on Saturday night.

"What do you mean, dance?" I asked.

"You know…boys, girls, emphasis on girls, music, dancing, etc., etc."

Darrell wore a larger than usual smile.

I started making excuses. "I don't think I should go, you know. I'm really in a good part of my Tarzan book…"

"What!?!" Darrell screamed, laughing. "You'd rather read a book than go to a dance with girls? You've been in here too long. You *have* lost your mind!"

I couldn't think of any other excuses. Then Darrell asked me, "Have you ever been to a dance?"

"Nope, never. Darrell, I'm only eleven years old." I replied.

Darrell smiled and said, "Don't worry about it. You'll love it. Everything will be fine. You'll see."

I wanted so much for there not to be a Saturday that week;

but, sure enough, it came—and a lot faster than usual. Clark could tell that I didn't want to go, but he said it would be a blast, and that everyone always has a good time. Plus, he was bringing two tons of cupcakes and lemonade. That evening Clark gave Darrell and I brand new short sleeve shirts and Levi's. He told us that he wanted us to "look good" that night.

As we prepared to leave the dorm, Darrell went to his locker and came out with what he referred to as "smell good." He patted some on his face, and then said, "Come here and see," and he patted some on my cheeks. "Guaranteed to make the girls' hearts melt," he added joyfully.

"But if their hearts melt, won't they die?" I joked.

He laughed and said, "They're just *dying...*to meet *you!*"

"Yeah, right!" I thought.

As we got in line to leave the unit, Darrell nudged me kind of hard with an elbow in the side and said, "Boy, are you going to love this!"

"Ooooh!" I resounded as I grabbed my side. "I do hope so!" I said.

Clark came down the line of kids and said, "Well, don't you

guys look swell!"

We all smiled at each other. "Thanks Clark!" we chimed.

The dance was in the cafeteria in the building across the way. We entered single file, hearing music playing, and noticed the lights dimmed somewhat. The girls quickly grabbed guys out of line to go to the dance floor with them. Just inside, I grabbed Darrell's arm, pulled him out of line, and ran toward a wall.

"What?" Darrell asked, "What's the matter?"

I told him, "Darrell, the girls are grabbing guys out of line to dance with them."

"Yes. We're the visiting team. They're the home team. You know, Sadie Hawkins. That's why the sign says 'Sadie Hawkins dance tonight.' What's your problem?"

"Who's Sadie Hawkins anyway?" I asked.

"Who cares? C'mon," Darrell said, looking at a group of girls across the room.

"Darrell, I've got something to tell you."

Darrell was waving at a group of really cute girls who were

pointing at us. Darrell waved and then looked toward me and said, "Look, don't blow this. I know these girls, and one of them likes me. What is the problem?"

"I've never danced before, Darrell. I don't know what to do."

"Eddie, my man, don't worry about a thing. Just do what I do, okay?"

Looking back in the direction of where the cute girls were, my heart suddenly just took off on its own, pounding like a drum. Oh, no! They were walking toward Darrell and me...four of them, all smiling and such, with their cute little dresses and shiny little shoes. I felt a rush of heat flush my face. Darrell nudged me in the side and said, "If your cheeks get any redder, they're gonna think you're a stop sign."

As the girls got closer, I could barely hear the music because my heart was pounding so loudly.

"Darrell, they're almost here. What do I do?" I asked frantically.

Darrell nudged me harder with his elbow in the side and said, "Be cool. Take it easy. They don't bite, you know—at least not on the *first* date!"

I tried to laugh, but nothing came out. My eyes must have been as big as silver dollars, and I'm almost positive my chin was resting on top of my tennis shoes as they arrived in front of us. One of them said, "Hi, Darrell. Who's your cute little friend? He's so cute."

One of them touched my cheek (which was probably as red hot as it looked) and said, "I'm Karen. What's your name, pretty boy?"

I tried to say something, but my mouth wouldn't close, my brain suddenly fled to hide in my back pocket, I think, and my heart pounded wildly as I stood there, all alone in front of the cutest little girl I'd ever seen.

She had the prettiest brown eyes with long eyelashes, long brown hair that just shined like gold, and medium brown skin that looked soft and smooth. Darrell looked at me and shook his head, telling her, "This is my best friend, Eddie. He's kind of new here, but he's not crazy. His mom just hates him, and usually he talks very well. I'm not sure what's wrong with him now."

Karen looked into my eyes with those fantastically bright, beautiful eyes of hers, and said to Darrell, "I know what's wrong with him! He's shy!" She then leaned toward me so close that I could smell how clean her pretty brown skin was, and she kissed my cheek!

The space my brain used to occupy between my ears immediately exploded. My heart beat so hard that it broke away from its hinges and fell into my stomach in a clump. Without a functioning brain, I couldn't breathe because my lungs didn't remember to inhale. My knees turned from bone and flesh to jelly and water, and I almost fell over. Karen grabbed both of my hands and whispered in my ear, "Let's go dance." Of all the boys there, this angel from heaven had just asked me to dance with her. Double WOW!

She took my hands to lead me out to the dance floor. Unfortunately, my absent brain didn't give my feet the message to follow, so I fell straight to the floor. All the girls laughed, of course, including Karen; but her beautiful eyes let me know, "It's okay."

Darrell helped me up, and I brushed off the front of my shirt and pants. He said to Karen, "Although he's acting totally retarded, he's not. Really. He's my best friend and I've never seen him like this."

Karen smiled as we continued on our way to the dance floor. She winked at me as she said, "We know what's wrong, huh? You've never danced with a girl before, have you?"

I must have swallowed my tongue or something because she made me so nervous that I couldn't say anything. I was able to shake my head no, with a silly grin on my face.

We got to the dance floor, and Darrell nudged me and said, "Watch this." He started doing a dance called the Hitch Hike. I watched for a second and could tell it was totally easy, so I looked at Karen, smiled, and started dancing! Me, dancing across from this pretty little angel of a girl and really enjoying it! Imagine that. And I stayed on my feet, too! I was soon able to relax and actually talk with her. I told her what a great dancer she was. She blushed a little and said, "Thank you. You're getting better yourself."

After a few more dances she drew me close and whispered in my ear, "You wanna get some lemonade and cupcakes?"

"Yeah, sounds good to me," I said.

As we walked over to the punch table Karen grabbed my hand and held it all the way from the dance floor to the refreshments.

Clark was at the cupcake table when he saw Karen and me. "Well, well, what do we have here? Who's your new friend,

Karen?" He smiled and gave a wink.

"Oh, hi, Clark. This is my new friend Eddie. Isn't he cute? He's mine, and I'm not going to let any other girls dance with him!" Clark laughed his loud laugh, knelt down between us and, as we held hands, he pronounced us boyfriend and girlfriend. All I could do was blush, which made Clark laugh loudly. He said, "Why, Eddie, you're blushing." I think my smile was from ear to ear—literally!

Clark looked at Karen and said, "I've got some outstanding news for you, sweetheart. Tomorrow, you're going home."

Karen looked into his eyes and cried out, "What?"

Clark shook his head and said, "No, not home with your mom and dad. Home with your grandma and little sister in South Carolina! All the staff pitched in and we flew your grandma out here and got you a ticket to fly back with her tomorrow!"

"Oh, my God!" Karen shouted, then gave Clark a big, giant hug saying, "Thank you! Thank you so much!"

All the staff had gathered around Karen, who was crying tears of joy as she hugged each and every one of them. Darrell, who had been dancing with all three of Karen's friends at the same time (who'da thought?), heard the commotion and came over with them. He asked what was going on and, without taking my eyes off of Karen, I quickly explained. Her friends starting screaming and grabbed Karen, telling her how glad they were. Darrell gave her a big hug, too.

Karen then grabbed my hand and said, "Come on, let's go talk. I'm so excited."

We ran hand in hand to the other side of the cafeteria and found a couple of chairs. Sitting on the edge of my seat, facing her, I looked into her eyes as she explained.

"I'm so happy!! My grandma has been going to court to get custody of me. I can't believe it took her two years. I can't wait to see her. I love her *soooo* much, and she loves me like I was her own child, you know? And she lives on the other side of the country, so I will be far, far away from my mom."

"What's wrong with your mom?" I asked.

Karen got a serious look on her face and told me, "One night when I was asleep, I woke up to find my dad on top of me, touching me and trying to do nasty things to me. I started screaming as loud as I could and he ran out of my room. My mom saw him in the hall and asked him what was wrong with me. He said he didn't know, that maybe I was having a bad dream, so Mom asked me what was I screaming about. I told her what my dad had done, but he kept telling her that I was lying about him, that he had never come into my room. I *hate* that sick bastard!"

Karen had tears in her eyes as she continued, and I did too. I wiped her tears as she wiped mine.

I just couldn't believe that there was someone in this world who would want to hurt this sweet little girl. As we held each other's hands, she continued. "I kept telling Mom, but she said that I must have had a bad dream. I told her, 'No! No! He was all over me.' She got mad and told me that I was a liar and that he would never do anything like that to me because he's my dad, and he loves me. I told her he was a sicko bastard and that I never, ever wanted to see him again. She slapped my face and said I was never to say that again as long as I lived. I stayed awake all night. Early in the morning, I got dressed and left the house to go to school. I told the principal, who believed me. I told him that I never wanted to go back home. Never! Ever! The police said that, because I was only eight years old, no one would believe me in court. My sister was six, but she had wanted to sleep in Mom and Dad's bed, so she wasn't in our room when he did what he did. So, I had no witnesses."

"The police called Social Services, and told them that I

didn't want to go home, and they came, and picked me up. Social Services took me to a foster home, and filed charges against my dad. He kept denying what he'd done, and said that I was crazy. That's how I ended up in here. Somehow, my dad blocked my grandma from having custody of me, but she told me that she would never give up, and that she believed my story. Three months ago, my dad attacked my baby sister. He raped her! They found his semen in her! Then they put him in prison. My grandma spent all she had to come out here to get my sister. And now she's coming to get me out of here. My mom moved near the prison where my dad is so she could be close to him. I don't think she believed my sister, either. She blames us for telling on him, but he's sick in the head, you know? He should be in here!"

I couldn't believe what I was hearing! I told Karen how sorry I was that these terrible things had happened to her. Again, we wiped each other's tears. She asked why I was in here and I told her everything. Then Clark came up and sat on the floor in front of us. "Is this how you guys act when you get good news?"

"C'mon, you guys. Karen, you've got a whole new life in front of you, and you must, listen to me, you *must* forgive and forget! Forget about that night he attacked you. If you don't, he'll be attacking you every day for the rest of your life, in your mind. Let it go, both of you. Do you understand? If you don't forgive, it will fester inside you and grow into a monster that you won't be able to control, and then what will become of you?"

"Karen, you're going to finally get out of here tomorrow. Forget about this place and get on with your life. You're going to finally be with your grandma; and your sister really needs your love, not your hate, for your mom and dad. Your love will heal you and your sister. Get on with your life and do right by your grandma and your sister. Love them and love yourself. Okay? Okay? Now get happy! You're out of here. Give me a hug!"

Karen gave Clark a hug and kissed him on his cheek.

"You, too, Eddie," Clark said, "give me a hug."

I gave Clark a hug and then he told us the dance was over so we'd better get going. Karen looked into my eyes with her pretty brown eyes and said, "I'm going to be okay now, are you?"

"You bet," I said.

We hugged and guess what, she gave me a kiss. First on the

cheek, and then right on my lips!

My brain turned into a bowl of mashed potatoes and my knees turned into jelly again; and, yes, again, I embarrassed myself and fell straight to the floor. Laughing, Karen covered her mouth and then ran out of the room. Clark laughed, too, and reached out his big hand to pick me up off the floor.

"Man, you'd better leave these girls alone until you get older."

I smiled sheepishly as I brushed off the back of my pants.

"She's wonderful," was all I could say.

"That she is! That she is!" laughed Clark as we left the cafeteria to find Darrell rolling on the hallway floor, laughing his head off.

"You will never be a Casanova, Eddie," Darrell squeaked, still laughing.

"What's that?" I asked.

"See!!" Darrell laughed, "That's what I mean! Did you see me? I had three girls and you could barely handle one!" Darrell giggled.

"Yeah," I answered, "but mine was an angel. I'll never wash this cheek or these lips again," pointing to the cheek that was still burning with her kiss.

"C'mon, you guys, you two 'lady-killers' have a date in your beds, and don't stay up talking all night. We've got to get an early start tomorrow," Clark said.

As Darrell and I got ready for bed, Darrell asked me, "So how did you like the dance? Cool, huh?"

"Yeah, I guess so. Next time I think I'll try to stay on my feet more."

Darrell asked, "You remember what the girls said, 'you're so cute' and they called you a 'pretty boy'?"

"So?" I replied.

"Girls love cute little boys and they really liked you, so you caught them. Dig?" Darrell started laughing again, "Even though you didn't know what to do with them, you caught them and I reeled them in. This is a good thing. We can work as a team, you pull them, and I'll secure them. Didn't you see me dancing with all three of them? That was really out of sight. Darrell Biggers dances with three girls all at the same time and Eddie gets his first kiss and falls flat on his butt! News at 5:00, stay tuned!! Ha, ha, ha!"

I touched the cheek that she kissed. It was still burning. I licked my lips and could taste the sweetness of her lipstick. Wow! She kissed me on my lips. I fell onto my bed and just relished the moment. I remembered how good she smelled and how soft her lips felt and how beautiful her eyes were and how soft her voice was and….

"Hey, you nut!" Darrell squeaked, giggling like a bowl of Jell-O. "Would it be safe to say that you like girls now?"

"Well, I know *one* I really like," I answered.

"That's too bad. Out of all the girls at the dance, you picked the one who's leaving tomorrow," Darrell quickly pointed out.

"That's okay. I'm glad she's going to get out of this horrible place and rejoin her sister and grandma. She was so happy, she was crying. I'm really happy for her. She deserves a good life, you know?" I said.

Darrell got serious. "Yeah, I know what you mean. Her dad should be shot. That's what Clark and I were telling you. There are so many sick people in the world who don't care who they hurt or how long the hurt will affect their victims. She's a real sweetheart, and she didn't deserve that. I'm happy for her, too. I'm really glad that someone in her family loved her enough to believe in her and step up to the plate to ensure her a nice future. I don't have anyone else in my family, how about you?"

"Naw, nobody," I reflected. "If my dad won't come get me, I'm stuck here."

"I think your dad will come get you. Maybe he's just trying to get your mom together and it's taking awhile, you know? But I'll ask you again, did you see me out there on the dance floor? Did you see me?" Darrell was elated.

"Yes, Darrell. I saw you. You're the *man!*"

As we fell asleep, I thought about Karen being released in the morning, and thought, "She's just like me. She really doesn't belong here. What's wrong with parents? Darrell looks a little strange but he doesn't belong here either. She's so sweet; he's so smart. And me, what about me? Why does Mom hate me so? Why did she adopt me? Was it just to have someone to beat?"

Shortly after I fell asleep that night, I was awakened by someone screaming, "Blanket Party!!!"

Some poor kid was being beaten up by half the dorm. The way it works is this. A group of four will gently cover their sleeping victim completely with a blanket, tying down the four corners of the blanket on the bed posts and then they yell, "blanket party!" Then anyone else who wants to join the "party" can come and sock the poor kid who is helplessly tied under the blanket. Not only can he not identify his attackers, he cannot fight back from under the blanket. Some kids would even insert an apple, or a bar of soap into a long sock and swing this at the poor victim. It was horrible to watch, and even more frightening to listen to. The blows would just keep coming! The night staff would come running in with flashlights, but they were always too late. I thought, "This is just too horrible!! How cruel can these kids be? Don't they realize they can seriously injure someone by doing this?"

Darrell had warned me about "blanket parties," instructing me to stay on my bunk and to pretend like I was asleep. He said to identify the attackers would be suicide, especially to the night crew. Darrell would tell Clark the next day who the attackers were, but they would not know it was Darrell that told.

I would just pull the covers over my head and fear for the life of the poor kid that was being attacked. It was so horrible to listen to and then hear the poor kid crying in pain all night if he was not taken to the infirmary. There would be at least one blanket party a week in this wicked place. I'm just glad Darrell and I were not ever one of the victims.

Clark got us up real early and taught us "breakfast to go."

"Watch and learn, gentlemen. Take a pancake, hold it in your hand like this, now spoon in some eggs, bacon, a little syrup, roll it up and *voilá*. Now we're out of here!"

Munching as we ran to keep up with Clark, Darrell managed in between bites to ask, "Hey Clark, where are we going?"

"It's a surprise. I want you both to see something nice, but don't talk. Okay?"

We both agreed and quickly gobbled our "breakfasts to go" as we continued to follow Clark. Once outside, we went over to the girls' unit. That's when Clark knelt down to speak to us.

"Okay, guys, I need you both to stand right here for a few minutes. Don't run off playing or anything, just stand here just as you are. Wait for me, okay?"

"Yes, Clark," we said together, and Clark went inside. We

did as Clark instructed and didn't even move an inch. In a few minutes, Clark returned carrying two suitcases and guess who was a few steps behind him. Yes, Karen. She was just as pretty as a flower.

And then a taxi pulled up and an older woman got out. Karen squealed, and ran toward the woman, and jumped into her arms, both of them crying. Karen said, "I love you, Grandma," and Karen's grandma replied, "Oh, child, I love you, too. I love you, too. I'm so glad you're okay. You look so pretty, child. I love you! Do you hear me? I love you so much. Thank God you're okay! Girl, you just don't know how much I've prayed for this day!"

"Grandma, I've missed you so much and I've prayed for you, too, and I love you so much. I prayed every night that this day would come. Ohhh, Grandma. Thank you for all you've done for me."

Clark gave them his handkerchief and wiped his own wet eyes with the back of his hand. Darrell had tears running down his cheeks. And me? Yeah, I was a wreck, too. There were five human beings crying their eyes out that early morning, yet not one of us was sad or hurt. Wow, tears of complete joy. *Joy!* Something I knew nothing about. Something I had never felt before.

Clark put Karen's luggage in the trunk of the taxi as Karen and her grandma got in the back seat. Karen's grandma wrapped both arms around Karen, who had to be sitting in her lap. Clark leaned into the car and they were talking for a little while. Karen and her grandma both gave Clark a kiss on his cheek and he got out of the car and closed the door.

Karen looked toward Darrell and me, brought her hand up to her lips, kissed it, and, like she was holding her kiss in her hand, blew it twice toward us. Darrell acted as if her kiss had been a bullet that struck him in the heart. He fell over backwards and kicked his feet up into the air. I put my hand to my cheek and waved good-bye. She quickly waved, smiled, and then laid her head on her grandma's chest, and the taxi took off into the morning.

As Clark came up to us, Darrell and I quickly wiped our tears with the fronts of our shirts.

"Well, Kiddos, what did you learn?"

Darrell answered first. "That Karen's got people other than her parents who love her and want to care for her?"

"Yeah, that's a great answer, but not the one I'm looking for. Eddie?"

"Is it that you can be so happy that it makes you cry?" I answered.

"Exactly! It's called tears of joy. I just wanted to show you both that, because of all the tears you've cried, but in pain. I wanted you to see that there are also other tears, tears of joy." Clark explained.

"Thank you, Clark," Darrell replied. "I almost forgot what it felt like. This was such a great morning, especially for Karen. I'm so happy for her."

Clark grabbed us both by our shoulders and, as we started walking back to our unit, he said, "Good. I'm glad you both got something out of this. Now *I'm* really hungry, so how about if we go finish breakfast?" Yeah!!

CHAPTER 19: MITZI

One time, using the payphone outside the unit, I called my dad and he answered the phone himself. He told me that Mitzi had died. He said that she had gotten too old and that she had been put to sleep. He also said that he had replaced her with another dog that I would really like. A German Shepherd, named Queenie. He said she was big and loved to play. When he hung up the phone, my knees gave way and I plopped down on the ground at the base of that payphone and just cried.

Mitzi dead? How could this be? Lassie never died. Rin Tin Tin never died. When I was a child, Lassie and Rin Tin Tin were dogs from television shows that I would watch. As talented as these TV dogs were, Mitzi had my heart. She was my best friend. How could she even know what had happened to me? I wondered if she thought I didn't love her anymore and had just left and deserted her. I missed her so much, being so far away, locked up here at Camarillo State Hospital. Oh my Mitzi!! I was so hurt and confused. Did her dying hurt? Was she in pain? Had she missed me as much as I missed her? Was it my leaving her, that killed her?

I remembered all the times we played in the backyard. Every day she would greet me with barks and yelps. She would stand on her back feet and knock me over and then lick my cheeks as I was lying on the ground beneath her. I would laugh and wrestle her to the ground. I would scratch her behind her ears and just above her tail on her back. She really liked that. She would roll over on her back and kick her feet as I rubbed her tummy. She especially loved it when I would brush her hair. She would lick my hand as I brushed her.

I would take her for walks in our neighborhood and allow her to stop and sniff and tinkle and do all the things she liked to do, as she pleased, at her own pace. She was great at chasing birds and butterflies. Never caught any, but she would let them know who was the queen of this jungle. Onyx, the Turners Great Dane, loved Mitzi. I think he had a crush on her. He would bark and jump whenever we walked by. Mitzi would just keep walking, not even concerned, with her nose in the air, like, "And?"

I remember a couple of times when my mom would come out of the house screaming and begin to beat the snot out of me. Mitzi would bark at her and growl. Even Mitzi knew that what my mom was doing to me was wrong. My mom even told my dad about how Mitzi was growling at her, but he refused to get rid of Mitzi. Boy! Was I glad!!

And now!! My Mitzi was dead! A piece of me died also, that lonely afternoon in Camarillo. I felt like I had really let her down. She had always been there for me, licking my wounds, as well as my tears. But now at her worst moment, I was a prisoner, so far away from her, helpless to do anything to comfort her. As I cried, I wondered, if I could have been there, would I have been able to comfort her? Perhaps even as I brushed her coat, I could have whispered in her ear, "It's going to be alright. You are going to a better place."

Would she have really believed me? Could I have given her any comfort with *my* words when I was so very afraid of dying myself? What's really out there waiting for us when we die? Where did Mitzi go? Will I ever get to see her again? Will she remember me? Oh! I felt so lost! It hurt so much! Why do we have to die? Mitzi loved me and I loved her, and now I was a prisoner in the most horrible place imaginable, and she was dead. I just sat in a heap and cried.

I heard a kind voice say, "How can I help?" It was Darrell, and Clark was right beside him. I looked up, tears running down my cheeks and said, "My dog is dead. Mitzi is dead."

Darrell and Clark both sat on the ground next to me, one on each side, and they each put an arm around my shoulders. I shared my grief, with them both listening quietly. I told them all I could remember about Mitzi.

Clark then shared a sad story about his favorite dog when he was a kid. His dog also had to be put to sleep because of old age. Darrell shared the loss of his puppy when the wind blew the gate of their backyard open and the puppy got out and was hit by a car. The puppy died in Darrell arms.

After Darrell shared his story, we all just sat there a few minutes in silence. Then Clark spoke these words. "You know, dogs were created by God, to be one of man's best friends. Isn't it amazing how they can capture our hearts? There is a special part of God that you can see and feel in animals. That special part is *love*. You know, when a puppy gives you his heart, he truly loves you, unconditionally. Even when you leave them, they get so excited when you return. Even if you spank them trying to potty train them, oh, how quickly they forget and come back in a few minutes licking, playing, and sharing their love. Dogs really know how to share love. We as people could learn so much from these supposed, 'dumb animals.' I think we underestimate them. They are a lot smarter than some people I know. And their love is pure, like straight from Heaven, and I know a lot of people that should be trying to love like this. If only we loved each other, as dogs love us, and we love them."

Darrell started to cry. Clark asked him why he was crying. Darrell answered, wiping his tears with the front of his shirt, "This little boy Eddie, got more love from a dog, than his own mother! That's a darn shame! My parents are more concerned about my appearance, than the love in my heart, and the love they should be sharing with me. Half the people in this place are here because no one loves them enough to care for them. Look at the 'gang.' They are blind, so what? They are filled with love and aren't afraid to show it! We hug them all day long and they love it! Even they have love to share. There should be a class where love is taught. There is just too much hate and cruelty in this world."

Clark wiped Darrell's tears with the back of his big strong hand and replied, "There is a class where love is taught. It's called 'life.' *Love* is a choice. People have this choice to make all day long. Every day they are given a chance to love others. What they choose to do with that chance is totally up to them. But I will say one thing, it feels so much better to love, than it does to hate."

Clark excused himself and said he'd be right back.

Darrell told me how sorry he was about Mitzi. I told him how awful it must have been to have had a little puppy die in his arms. Darrell admitted how helpless he felt as his puppy slowly died in his arms. Darrell said all he could do was cry and just kiss his puppy until he breathed his last breath. Wow! He kissed him into eternity!

Clark came back with a football. We all played catch and laughed as we played. We spent that whole afternoon outside playing with each other. Darrell was a riot to watch as he ran. As unorthodox as it looked, he was having a blast! We walked around the whole place and even went bowling with Clark. Clark was amazed at how good we were bowling and thanked Floyd with a hug for all he had been doing for Darrell and I.

That night, and the next, I joined the rest of the children that cried themselves to sleep at night. I cried for the greatest dog that had ever lived. I cried for Mitzi, who truly loved me with all of her heart.

CHAPTER 20: DARRELL GOES HOME FOR A VISIT

A couple of days later, Darrell's parents came to get him, to spend a week at home with them. Clark told me that he was going to take a few days off and invited me to come and stay at his home with his family. He was such a great father and husband. His two boys and I played baseball together and I slept in their room with them. They took me right in and Clark's wife really treated me as one of the family. On the third day away from the hospital, Clark got a phone call. He said we would have to return quickly. Darrell was having a problem with his parents, and would be back to the hospital shortly. Clark wanted us to be there when Darrell arrived.

On the way back to Camarillo State Hospital, I thanked Clark again and told him that I loved his two boys and wife. I told him that his family was just beautiful and what a wonderful daddy he was. I also told him how I wished my family was like that. "Never give up hope, Kiddo," Clark said. "You never know what tomorrow may bring."

We arrived just a few minutes after Darrell had, and we found him on his bunk, crying his little heart out. Clark and I ran over to his bunk and I patted Darrell on his back and told him I was there, and that I loved him. He turned over, got up and grabbed Clark in a hug, and just cried. "I never want to go back, never again!"

I sat on the edge of Darrell's bunk as he started to explain what had happened.

"My mom and dad threw a dinner party last night. I was told not to come out of my room. My brother and sister were downstairs at the party, and no one realized that I had not eaten since breakfast. I was so hungry that I thought I would see if I could sneak downstairs and grab something to eat and get back upstairs without anyone seeing me. I could not believe my ears when I heard what my mother was saying about me to some friends of hers. Apparently my brother had slipped and told another kid that he had an older brother. This kid told his mom who was asking my mom, 'I thought you said you had a child that died at birth? Didn't you say he died from some sort of birth defect?' My mom answered, 'Oh yes, he died years ago, we just keep him alive in our hearts so his brother and sister will know that they had an older brother. He was so precious to us and we still miss him.' I wanted to throw up I was so mad!! I couldn't believe what my mom was saying about me!"

Darrell took a couple of deep breaths and continued. "I came out of my hiding spot and walked over to the buffet table and started making a plate. I asked her, "Dead Mom? Is that what I am to you now? Are you so ashamed of how I look that you told all your friends that I am dead?" The party stopped as everyone started looking at me, and then my mom. I told her right there in front of them all that I was not dead, and that I was a genius, and that she had hidden me away in Camarillo State Hospital with a bunch of crazy people and child molesters. My mom screamed and asked me why I had come out of my room. I told her that she had forgotten to feed her dead son. I finished making my plate and as I went back up to my room, I asked her to bring me back here to the hospital. I told her I never wanted to come home again. She paid for a cab to bring me this morning."

There were tears in Clark's eyes, as he listened to this horrible story. I was crying too. I hid my face as I pulled my shirt up to dry my tears. Poor Darrell. He was so wonderful, and my best friend. I felt so sorry for him.

As Clark held onto Darrell, he said softly, "Awwww, Kiddo, I'm so sorry. That is just terrible. I wish I could do or say something that would make all this go away. I really do. You don't deserve this Darrell. But you have got to keep your chin up. I know it's hard, but you just can't give up. You are so young, and your whole life is in front of you. You are going to be somebody great one day, someone really great and wonderful. You are great now, you are a really great kid. Just wait until you grow up. Then they will all see. Don't let this stop you Darrell. Eddie and I are rooting for you."

Darrell wiped his tears with the front of his shirt and stood up proudly and said, "I will not give up! I will live and be just as great as I can be! I will! I promise you!!"

With tears in my eyes, I gave Darrell the biggest hug and told him I loved him and that he was the greatest right now. I told him that he was the greatest friend a kid could ever hope to have and that one day, the world would see it for itself.

Clark allowed us both to go outside and play and run and do anything we wanted. He didn't even charge us the ten tokens each to get out. In fact he gave us both a handful of tokens and we bowled all day.

Chapter 21: I'm Going Home?

About two weeks later, I received the news. Clark caught Darrell and me coming in from bowling one afternoon. "Eddie, I've got great news! I just hung up the phone from talking to your dad!"

"My dad?" I asked.

"Yes, your dad called while you guys were out bowling. He said to get you packed and ready, 'cause he'll be here early in the morning to pick you up. You're outta here, Kiddo!"

I couldn't believe my ears! Finally!! *Finally* I was going home. I jumped up into Clark's arms and he swung me around as I kept thanking him for all he had done for me. "Thank you so much, Clark. Thank you! *Thank you!* **Thank you!**"

I hugged Darrell so hard he squeaked and when I looked in his eyes he was crying. "I'm sorry! Did I hurt you?" I asked.

Darrell said, "Tears of joy!" as he wiped his tears. "I told you. I knew you'd get out of here," Darrell said behind a big grin.

"Wow!" I screamed. "Yes! I'm going home!"

Clark was grinning from ear to ear. "This day I'll always

remember! I'm so happy for you. And you be good, and always remember us."

"I could never forget this place or how the two of you really took care of me. I'll never forget you!" I said. "You're the best friends a kid could ever have."

Darrell and I went to find the Gang. I told them my good news and got lots of hugs. Darrell helped me pack that night and gave me a Tarzan book, which he signed, "To the best friend I ever had. Don't forget me. Darrell."

The next morning, Clark got us up and we went to breakfast. At breakfast, Clark told me, "No matter what happens, always know you've got two friends who love you, and there will always be someone who's doing worse than you. It can never get worse than this place, so know that you're going uphill."

Before we finished breakfast, my dad was escorted into the staff cafeteria. I ran up to him and gave him the biggest hug and introduced him to Clark and Darrell. My dad thanked them for taking care of me and said, "Okay, let's go. We've got a long drive ahead of us."

I gave Clark and Darrell a last goodbye hug. Then I grabbed my suitcase and—finally!—followed my dad out of the

Camarillo State Hospital's mental ward.

As we got to the car, I noticed Mom in the front seat and my brother and sister in the back seat. "Hi, Mom," I said. She said absolutely nothing. She looked at me as if I were a cow turd. I was shocked at her response, or the lack of one, and my dad had to tell me to get in the car.

As I got in the backseat, my brother and sister were looking straight ahead like something was wrong. Oh boy, I thought. "It doesn't look like anything has changed with Mom. And my brother and sister aren't acting like it was good to see me, and nobody's saying anything at all". I'd hoped that someone would have been glad to see me. I was sure glad to see all of them. As my dad kept driving along, nobody said a word.

"So what's wrong?" I asked to anybody who would answer. No one answered; however, Mom did turn her head to look at me as if I were a pile of vomit sitting on the backseat. I nudged my brother and looked at him with a "what's going on?" look on my face. He just shrugged and continued to look straight ahead. I was so deflated I just sat there in disbelief. I was so happy that my dad had come to get me and now I thought, "What's going on with these people? What's wrong with this picture? Oh well, maybe after we get home I can find out from my brother what's really going on."

Finally, we reached Los Angeles on the 10 freeway; but Dad didn't get onto the 405, or get off on La Brea Avenue or Crenshaw Boulevard. As we approached downtown L.A., I tapped my dad on the shoulder. He looked at me in the rear view mirror and said, "Yes?"

I said, "You missed the turn to go home, didn't you?"

"No, I didn't miss the turn. We're not going home."

Gulp!

"We're not? Then where are we going?" I asked.

"Just sit back and be quiet. We'll be there in a couple of hours," my dad said quietly.

"We'll be *where* in a couple of hours? Am I not going home with you guys?" I asked quietly.

"You are *not* going home with us," Mom screamed at me, "and if I have anything to do with it, you will *never* come home with us!!"

My dad told her not to start, and told us to just be quiet. After about 10 or 15 minutes, I asked, "Why can't I go home? I want to go home."

My mom was ready to explode and my dad looked at her and told her not to say one word. "You can't come home with us, Eddie. It just won't work. Your mom needed time to find somewhere else for you to go, that's why we didn't come to get you sooner. You are just going to have to deal with it. You can't come home. You just can't," my dad explained.

Back at Camarillo, when I ran up to my dad and gave him the biggest hug I could, I noticed then that he hadn't hugged me back. In fact, he had to pull me off of him before he said, "Let's go. We've got a long drive in front of us."

I guess I was just so excited to see my dad that it just did not register to me at that time. I was starting to get the picture now as he was speaking to me in the car. You know how I felt? I felt like an eleven-year-old kid who'd just had a 110-foot, rusty, galvanized, 2" pipe thrust into his heart, and pulled through slowly. All 110 feet! A very rusty and nasty pipe. With corrosion and nicks and cuts in the metal.

My mom turned to look at my hurt. I could tell from her eyes that she was gloating. My dad told her to turn around and face the front and leave me alone. I had forgotten how much I hated her until she gave me that look. I had hoped that the war to exterminate little Eddie had been over and forgotten. But at that moment, that gleam in her eyes let me know it had only just begun. The Wicked Witch of the West was still hell bent on getting me killed, or at least out of their lives. Okay, Witch, one day, when you least expect it, it will be your blood, not mine...your blood spilling on the carpet. One day, you Witch, one day. Don't forget, I know where you live.

I sat there thinking to myself that of all the families I could have been born into, why this one? Oh, yeah, I'm adopted. Well, I wondered, what were my real parents like? Better? Worse? Dead? Did they have any idea what I was going through? Did they care? Why was I born anyway? What would become of me? Does my dad really love me?

Who are these people anyway? How can Dad just sit there and drive and let her do this to us? What's wrong with him anyway? As mean as she is, he loves her more than me? What "wonderful" place has she picked out for me now? I survived Camarillo State Hospital, thanks to Clark and Darrell, but will I survive this next place? How long will I be there this time? I hate the air she breathes, that keeps her alive. Why can't she just die right now so that we can be a family? *Die, you witch!!!*

If only she would just die!

I thought about Clark and Darrell. Did they know that I wasn't going home? What were they doing right now? I wished I were still there. Where was the Gang, and what were they doing?

It was getting really hot and I looked up and we were in the desert, nothing but miles and miles of sand. A few hills, some mountains in the background, and sand as far as you could see in any direction.

The windows were down but the air was so hot that we were all miserable. I was sweating and so were my brother and sister. I could see the sweat on their foreheads. I could see the sweat on the back of my dad's neck as he said, "God, it's hot out here." And it only got hotter.

My shirt was soaking wet when we finally got there. My dad said that it had to be 115°. It was hotter in this place than anyplace I'd ever known. The air was hard to breathe and the heat was intense.

My dad parked in front of a fairly new, good-looking building with almost black windows and told me to get out of the car. We went to the trunk and I grabbed my suitcase and, under a blanket, was a new one. My dad said to take that one, too. They were both heavy and, by the time I got them out of the trunk, he was talking to someone dressed like a Catholic priest, robes and all.

"All right then, we'll see you," my dad said as he got back into the car, started the engine, and took off across the desert.

No hug, no good-bye, no "luv ya"—just gone.

I stood there holding both suitcases, tears streaming down my cheeks which were already wet with sweat.

I watched him drive away, as if he had left no one behind.

CHAPTER 22: WELCOME TO BOYS TOWN

"So, tell me, young man, what do you see?" this priest asked me. I looked up to look at his face. He was big, he was black, and he looked mean.

"Sir, I see my family leaving me," I answered.

"Good," he smiled. "Do you know what that means?"

"No, Sir."

"That means that you belong to me now. What else do you see?"

I looked around, "Nothing but sand, Sir."

"Correct. You are in the middle of the desert, 25 miles from the closest town. In this heat, you couldn't walk more than five miles before the heat would kill you."

He pointed out around the building and said, "That way is the way to town. Those ways," he said, pointing off in other directions, "go nowhere for hundreds of miles. If you look closer, you will see that there are no gates; no fences to stop you from running away; no guards. You are free to run away anytime you want to; however, if you live, we will add another year to your time. Do you want to run away?"

"No Sir."

"Good. Come on inside and I'll explain where you are."

He handed me a brochure as we went inside and sat down in his office. This building was so nice with marble floors, lots of wood, and ice-cold air conditioning.

"My name is, and all you will ever call me is, Brother Bernard. You are in Boys Town of the Desert. Have you ever heard of Father Flanagan of Boys Town in Omaha, Nebraska?"

"No Sir."

"Father Flanagan had a ranch full of orphans, and 'He ain't heavy, he's my brother' was his motto. You are in Beaumont, California, and, believe me, there are kids in here who are *not*, and I repeat, *not* your brothers."

"Boys Town is a kind of half-way place between Juvenile Hall and home; or between home and Juvie. It depends which way you are traveling. Judges will also sentence children here to see how they do before sending them on to prison or Juvenile Hall. Most of these kids have already done many years in Juvie and should, or could, go home in a year or two, depending on how they act here. Any questions so far?"

"Yes Sir. How long am I here for?" I asked not really wanting to hear the answer.

"Dunno. Two, three, four years. You aren't sentenced like they are. Whenever your parents feel like coming to get you, I guess. Do you know *why* you are here?"

"No Sir."

"Your mother says that you are totally out of control and that you frighten her with your fits of rage."

Fits of rage? When did I ever have a fit of rage? I just sat there in disbelief of the newfound lies my mother had come up with to get me into this hellhole.

Brother Bernard was looking at my file and he asked me, "Who is Clark?" I asked Brother Bernard if there was a phone number for Clark. He said yes, there was. I simply said, "If you want the truth about me and my mom, call Clark."

I couldn't believe what happened next. Brother Bernard picked up the phone and called Clark. Yes! Please Clark, be there.

He was. "Hello, yes. Hang on." Brother Bernard gave me two quarters and told me to go back to the lobby and get us each a soda from the machine. I asked him if I could talk to Clark.

Brother Bernard said, "Before I hang up, you can say hi. Now go and do what I asked."

I went to the soda machine and got two Cokes and when I got back to his office, Brother Bernard's door was closed, but I could hear him talking through the door, saying, "What you say! You've got to be kidding me, right?"

I thought, "Tell him Clark, don't leave anything out. Maybe," I thought, "just maybe Clark will come and get me."

After about an hour Brother Bernard opened the door and told me to pick up the phone. "Hello," I said.

"Hey, Kiddo. I'm so sorry. I thought you were going home too. I'm so sorry. I told Brother Bernard there all about your situation. He knows everything that I know, but listen to me, Kiddo. You're in a different kind of place now and there's nothing else I can do to help you. You've got to be tough and hang in there and just remember that Darrell and I are pulling for you. You can make it, you hear me? You can make it. Now step up to the plate and be tough and don't back down, you hear?"

"Yes, Clark. I hear you. I will. I promise. I'll be tough, just like you. I miss you already. Will I ever see you again?"

Clark hesitated and then said, "Naw, Kiddo, I don't think so. I'm here and you're there, but you'll always be in my heart. Keep me and Darrell in yours, and fight like hell, okay?"

"Okay, Clark. I will."

Dial tone. I just stood there trying to figure out what he had just told me.

Brother Bernard took the phone from me and hung it up and asked me, "Will you take off your shirt and turn around so I can see your back?"

I did as he requested and it seemed like forever as he looked at my scars. I turned around as Brother Bernard was wiping a tear from his eye and he quickly said, "That's absolutely terrible. Put your shirt back on. I've seen and heard enough."

Brother Bernard got up from behind his desk and stood with his back to me and looked out the window for a while. I finished my soda not knowing what to say or do, but I said, "Brother Bernard?"

"Yes, Eddie?"

"Here's your soda, Sir."

He laughed and said, "Thanks, I forgot all about it."

He sat back down. I asked him what he was looking at out the window. He told me, nothing, that he was praying.

"Praying?"

"Yes," he told me. "I was asking the Lord, what I could do with you."

"Sir, what did the Lord say?" I asked, wondering if he was really talking to the Lord.

"He said that you were not supposed to be here. He said that this place is not for you."

"Good. I believe Him," I said, "I've never even seen a Juvenile Hall. Is it really bad?"

Brother Bernard looked at me and said, "You've got no idea how bad it is, but understand this, most of those kids are here."

"So, did the Lord say I could leave?" I asked hoping there was a way out of this mess.

"No, child. I'm sorry, but you're here to stay. My job is to keep you alive while you remain here. That's what the Lord said. Keep this child alive."

"Is it that bad?" I asked, not wanting to hear the answer, but needing to know what Mom had got me into.

"It's that bad, and then some. Tell me about Clark."

I told him that Clark was my best friend who had helped and protected me, and taught me things, and went on and on until I ran out of words.

Brother Bernard just looked at me and listened. When I finished telling him about Clark, he said to me, "Look, kid, I can't protect you like he did; and you can't tell anyone in here that you were in the Camarillo State Hospital. You tell them that you ran away from a foster home, okay? You being in here is like throwing a lamb into a lion's cage. You mustn't tell anyone what I tell you, and you are going to have to protect yourself. You've got to be tough as nails, and you can never let them see you cry."

"I'm going to take you on a tour and I'm going to put you in Brother Matthew's Cottage. You're only eleven, and so that's the age group of Brother Matthew's Cottage. It's called Cottage A. That's where we have the 8-year-olds to 13-year-olds.

Cottage B has the 14- to 15-year-olds; Cottage C, the 16- to 17-year-olds; D, the 18- to 19-year-olds; and E, the 19- to 22-year-olds."

"Brother Matthew is a friend of mine. We were in the monastery together. I can trust him and let him know who you really are and why you are here. You'll like Brother Matthew."

"Well, it's time for you to grow up, and I mean quickly. Like five minutes ago. C'mon. Let me show you Boys Town of the Desert."

As we walked, he talked on his walkie-talkie to different people. The building we left also contained the chapel and the cafeteria. Breakfast, lunch, and dinner were held in the cafeteria at different times for each cottage. Chapel was every day after lunch. The school classrooms were to the left and down the hill. Fantastic! There's a baseball field and a football field!

Up and over the hill and down were the cottages with A being first and E last. A winding asphalt road and cement walkways connected them all. They were beautiful buildings made of brick and dark wood beams with rock faces at the doors, and smoked glass windows and skylights. As we approached Cottage A, Brother Matthew came out and met us on the walkway.

Brother Matthew was tall and thin and black, with glasses. Of the 20 or so priests, only these two were black, but all of the priests got along and highly respected one another.

Brother Bernard grabbed and hugged Brother Matthew and didn't let go. I'd have thought it strange, but I could see Brother Bernard whispering in Brother Matthew's ear.

"I'm sorry, Eddie. I want you to meet Brother Matthew.

Brother Matthew, meet Eddie Wiggins."

Brother Matthew had a great smile and he grabbed my hand and shook it like we were long time friends. "Welcome to Boys Town, and I'm really glad you're coming to Cottage A. We've been short a few kids and we really need your help. Every week we win the Cleanest Cottage Award and get to go to the movies in town. Do you like to clean?"

"Yes Sir, I do," I answered sheepishly.

"Oh, thank you, Jesus. Thank you, Lord!" Brother Matthew said, looking at the heavens as he said that. "We're going to get along fine. Just fine!"

Brother Bernard asked Brother Matthew to walk with us as we walked by all the cottages to the end of the road. Brother Bernard called into E unit and asked that a kid named Allen come outside. This 'kid' Allen was huge and black, with muscles coming out of his ears. He looked like anything but a 'kid.'

"Allen," Brother Bernard said, "This is Eddie, and he's one of yours, and I want you to take good, and I mean *good*, care of him."

I put my hand out to shake his hand and smiled, but I

guess he wasn't in the mood for shaking hands. He didn't totally ignore me, though. He reached down and, with one hand, grabbed me by the stomach and lifted me over his head. He held me there for a moment before putting me back on my feet and commenting, "Well, there's not a whole *lot* of you here, but hopefully you at least got heart. There are only five black kids here, and you make six. I protect all the black kids, and nobody here can whup me. I'm the King Kid, you got it?"

"Yes Sir," I squeaked.

"I ain't no sir, and you better get this. If anybody messes with you, you better not back down, and you better draw blood. You draw blood, I kill them. Even if you lose, you better draw blood. If you don't fight back, or if you run, or if you don't draw blood, I'll kill you myself. You got dat?!" Allen growled.

"Yeah, I got it. Draw blood. Yes Sir. I got it," I squeaked.

Allen grabbed me by the front of my shirt and picked me up to his height and said, "I ain't no sir! What's wrong with you?"

"Well, what should I call you?" I asked, hoping that I could keep my teeth, as well as get an answer.

161

"Everybody calls me Allen, or King Al! Now you got it?"

"Yes, Allen. King Al. Yes, I got it," I almost screamed.

As Allen set me back down to earth, to my great relief, he asked me how old I was. I told him, "Eleven years old, King Al." Then I added, "and I'll be twelve soon," hoping for his approval.

He just walked back to his cottage, shaking his head. Didn't say a word.

As I turned around to face Brother Bernard and Brother Matthew, they were both smiling. Brother Bernard asked me what I'd thought of King Al.

"I don't think he likes me very much," I answered.

"Oh, I think he likes you fine, Eddie." Brother Bernard sort of giggled. "He picked you up, twice. You should have hugged him. You were close enough."

"Uh-huh," I mumbled.

CHAPTER 24: WELCOME TO COTTAGE A

As we headed back to Brother Matthew's Cottage A, I saw another Brother delivering my luggage in a golf cart. Brother Matthew helped me take my luggage in and, as Brother Bernard left, he said, "God bless you, Eddie. Welcome to Boys Town."

I thanked him and went inside.

It was beautiful, clean beyond belief, ultra-modern and smelled excellent. Floors were shiny like mirrors, windows were tinted and spotless. It was like walking into a magazine picture of a home. Brother Matthew showed me around. In the front was the day room with chairs, couches, and TV. The kitchen was large and clean. Radio was piped through speakers in every room, controlled by Brother Matthew exclusively.

Brother Matthew showed me his room, which always remained locked unless he was in there and wanted it open. It was nice, with all the comforts of home. He had a lot of books and records: 33s, 45s—you know.

Brother Matthew's room had its own bathroom and shower and a refrigerator. Next to his room was the isolation room. He didn't open it, but told me to look through the glass.

It was a small room with a cot or a small bed. That was it.

"What's an isolation room?" I asked.

"That's where bad kids might have to go to keep them away from the group. You see, Cottage A is a family. I'm the daddy. If you don't obey Daddy, you won't be allowed to disrupt the family. The family always comes first. Period. You must always obey me and cooperate with me, and with the family. Failure to do so will require a sort of 'time out' or isolation period until the 'isolated' one decides to cooperate and rejoin the family. Understand?"

"Yes Sir," I answered.

Brother Matthew continued the tour. We got to the bedrooms where there were other children. Brother Matthew and I went into each of the four bedrooms and he introduced me to each and every one of them.

Each room could hold four kids. However, one room wasn't being used and there were two children in each of the three rooms that were occupied. All of the kids were white except for two, and I had no idea what they were, but everyone was nice and shook hands as we were introduced.

Brother Matthew announced that all the kids could go back

to doing whatever they wanted and, with a few yells, they were gone.

He told me that he had restricted each of the boys to their beds while he left the cottage to meet Brother Bernard and me. Brother Matthew showed me a whistle he wore around his neck and explained that, whenever I heard this whistle, it meant to line up or get on our beds; and, after he blew the whistle, he would tell us what he wanted us to do.

Brother Matthew showed me my bed, locker, dresser, and nightstand. He told me to go ahead and unpack, and that he would send in one of my roommates, either Steve or Pepe, to give me the 'family' rules.

As I unpacked and put my clothes away, the white kid Steve came in and said, "Hey, I'm Steve, one of your roommates. What's your name again?"

"Eddie," I said with a smile.

Steve was a cool kid about 12 years old. He had long hair that kept getting in his eyes, so he'd throw his head to the side to make his hair move out of his face.

"So what are you in here for? Did you come from Juvic?" Steve asked me.

"Naw, no Juvie. I ran away from a foster home." I lied, just as Brother Bernard had instructed me to.

"Why did you run away?" Steve quizzed me.

"I just didn't like it. You know, I wanted to go home to be with my dad." I hoped that would satisfy his curiosity, but Steve continued.

"So why were you put in a foster home in the first place?" Steve asked.

"My mom hates me and didn't want me anymore. You know, we just couldn't get along," I answered.

"So, what are you, black or what?" Steve continued his interrogation.

"Black," I answered.

My other roommate was standing in the doorway. Pepe was his name, and he came in and shook my hand and asked, "So, where did you run away from?"

"A foster home," I answered.

"No, man. Where was it? What city?" Pepe asked.

"Uhhh, Camarillo," I answered uneasily.

"Camarillo? There's nothing there but a nut house. Were you in the nut house?"

"No!" I insisted. "I was at a foster home."

"Groovy, man, no sweat!" Pepe answered, and left Steve and me alone in the room.

"What did he just say?" I asked Steve.

"He said, it's cool, don't worry about it."

"So you're black? You don't look black." Steve asked with a cool head jerk to move his hair from in front of his eyes.

"So what is Pepe, Japanese or something?" I asked.

"Did you call Pepe a Japanese or something? Hey, Pepe! Come here quick!"

As Pepe came in the room, with most of the other kids in the cottage trailing behind him, I knew that I had already blown it, however unintentionally. I could tell from Steve's change of attitude that one wrong thing said could be explosive around this camp.

"What's happening?" Pepe asked as he re-entered the room.

"This new kid called you Japanese or something," Steve said proudly, as if he had captured a wild tiger all by himself. With that, Steve snapped his head back and returned a toothpick to one side of his mouth and folded his arms across his chest.

"Way to go, Steve. You cocky SOB. You just stand right there and flick your long hair. I'll be with you as soon as I get through with Pepe," I thought. "Be tough, step up to the plate." I told myself. "You'd better draw blood," I remembered King Al had warned. My heart was racing and I knew what would come next.

"Okay, a**#~!, you called me a what? !#@," came out of Pepe's mouth just before my fist went in and busted both of his lips.

Pepe hit me hard in the face. I flew backwards, tripped over my bed, and landed on the floor on my back. Pepe was on top of me fast, attempting to smash my face. I had my arms blocking my face, but he got another blow in and smashed my nose. I got mad and scared at the same time and threw Pepe off me. He was attempting to stand up but I beat him to it.

That's when Steve grabbed me from behind, around my neck. I brought down my elbow and buried it in Steve's side.

168

He went straight to the floor gasping for air. Pepe swung and missed, and I socked him right in the eye. The blow brought him to his knees. I was raging and I wanted to finish Pepe off so I could get back to Steve.

Steve was still on the floor, trying to get his lungs to suck in some air. I started to swing my finishing blow to Pepe's face so I could kick the crap out of Steve, when I was picked up off the ground from behind.

As my feet left the ground, I heard Brother Matthew's whistle in my ear. "All right, it's over! Calm down! It's over! Nobody's going to hurt you! Calm down! Sit down on your beds all of you!" Brother Matthew commanded.

"Now then, who wants to tell me what happened here?" Complete silence.

Brother Matthew folded his arms and tapped his foot on the floor.

Then he said, "Pepe? I can just see by looking at you that you have something to tell me. Get up, look in the mirror!!"

Pepe got up and stood in front of the mirror. His right eye was swollen closed and turning black. His nose and mouth had dripped blood all over the front of his face and down the front of his neck and white T-shirt.

"Well, are you going to tell me now? Or would you prefer to sit in isolation for the rest of the week?" questioned Brother Matthew.

"He hit me first!" Pepe stated.

"Did he now?" asked Brother Matthew. "I can only wonder why."

"He called me a Japanese or something. You can ask Steve. He heard him," Pepe stated.

"Steve?" Brother Matthew looked Steve's way.

"Yep, that's what he said. Japanese or something," Steve quipped, still holding his side. His hair was all in his eyes, but no cool whip of the hair this time.

Next, Brother Matthew looked towards me. "Eddie, isn't there something you'd like to share with me?"

"Yes Sir. They, meaning Steve and Pepe, were asking me if I was black. I just asked Steve if Pepe was Japanese or something. I didn't say it to like hurt his feelings. We'd just met. They were curious about me, and I was curious about Pepe. I've never met anyone like him." I tried to explain.

"See! He said it again! See what I mean? I ain't no Japanese or something! I'm Mexican you know, a *cholo*! Haven't you ever seen a Mexican before? What kind of neighborhood do you live in?" Pepe argued.

Brother Matthew seemed to side with Pepe as he asked me, "Well, what kind of neighborhood do you come from?" I told them that the only kids in my neighborhood were black, and a few were white. I hadn't seen any Mexican kids in our neighborhood, not even at school.

"Well, there you go, Pepe," Brother Matthew continued, "He's never seen a Mexican until he met you. So what's wrong with that? And now that he's met his first Mexican, look what you did to him. Is this how you want him to feel about Mexicans? I believe you poorly represented your people, don't you?"

"Yes, Brother Matthew, you're right. But how could I possibly know that he'd never seen a Mexican?" Pepe asked. "Who's never seen a Mexican before?"

Brother Matthew said, "Pepe, have you ever met a Nigerian or an American Indian?"

"No Sir," Pepe answered.

"It's not a requirement that every child know the nationality of every child on earth. You can know only what you've seen or experienced for yourself. Don't be so anxious to judge if you meet someone who doesn't know you. A lot of people have no idea that you even exist. The world doesn't revolve around you. The world could care less about you. When God puts someone in your life, try to find out why and how it can be a good thing for both of you."

"Now, both of you stand in front of the mirror. Right now!"

We got up and stood side by side in front of the mirror. As we looked at ourselves, and each other, we both realized how awful we looked.

"Man, I'm really sorry," Pepe said to me.

"I'm sorry, too, Pepe," I said.

Brother Matthew had us shake hands and told us both to get cleaned up.

While we were in the bathroom washing off the blood, Pepe told me, "Man, I like you. You're skinny, but you fight like a Mexican. You got heart. We should be best friends and look out for each other, you know?"

"Yeah, man, I'd like that a lot. That would be cool with me," I said as I wiped my bottom lip, which was swollen beyond belief. My left eye was pretty sore and turning black.

One of the kids, Henry, ran into the bathroom and said, "That fool, Mad Dog, from C Cottage is on the row again!"

Pepe shouted to me, "C'mon!" All the kids in our cottage ran out the front door.

Let me explain what was happening "on the row." There was a crack in the cement that no kid was allowed to cross without a counselor. The only time you could cross this line was when your counselor was walking with you to march you to the cafeteria for mealtime, to chapel, to school, or to a bus for a field trip.

Now, you could go out the backdoor of the cottages and play, but you were on your own if you strayed too far. You'd want to stay as close to your cottage as you could—for 'safety.'

The 'fool' was the boy who would go out the front and 'walk the row,' then stop in front of a cottage to challenge it. All challenges had to be met, or your cottage would be terrorized by all the rest.

Since the cottage to your right was younger in age,

therefore 'weaker,' most challenges went to the right; however, a few challenges would go to the left, which was considered suicide! There was no cottage to our right, because we were the youngest in Boys Town.

There would usually be one kid who would challenge another cottage, and that cottage would send out their 'baddest.' As long as the challenge was met, respect remained throughout Boys Town. If your cottage sent no one out to meet the challenger, then the challenger had 'punked' your cottage and all the other cottages would ruin your lives forever.

To lose a fight was no big deal as long as you fought. If you fought some older kid and won, you got awesome respect! Not much credit went to older kids picking on younger kids. Counselors knew of course, but weren't condoning these contests.

For any kid to be on the row without a counselor was a violation and isolation for a week was mandatory. Since our cottage housed the youngest and smallest boys, Brother Matthew would usually chase the 'walker on the row,' and take him to his counselor for isolation. However, he told us to protect each other at all times, which meant that if our cottage or anyone in it was challenged, all of us were to go out together and, "Beat the hell out of them!"

We might have been the smallest group, but there were seven of us, all running and yelling at the top of our lungs, and seven against one generally means that the "one" was running away with a change of plans.

Right by the front door of each cottage was a small front patio, approximately 4' by 4'. This area was okay for standing or smoking, but don't cross the line in the cement leading down the cottage path, which puts you on the row.

Behind the cottages was nothing but sand, dirt trails, cacti, snakes, lizards, and a huge, wide, extremely hot desert.

Sometimes we'd go on field trips out into the desert. Hikes, we used to call them. All hikers went out through the backdoor.

And there were no rules in the back. You could visit other cottages—at your own risk, of course. You could 'shout a line,' that is, pass along information or gossip, mainly about fights or threats of future fights.

Back to the bathroom, Pepe was telling me that he was thirteen years old. He got busted for joyriding and commercial burglary with his older cousin who went to prison. They were in a gang, called the 18th Street, and warring with another gang called White Fence.

All of a sudden, Henry came in and said that Pepe had a challenger on the row. "It's Mad Dog!"

Mad Dog was a *cholo* from a couple of cottages up the row, C Cottage. Mad Dog was 17, with tattoos all over his arms, and he hated Pepe, who was the baddest of A Cottage. Pepe looked at me and said, "I can't beat him. Will you help me?"

"I'll pretend he's my mother. We'll kill him, Pepe!" I said.

As we all ran out the front door onto the row, with Pepe and me in front, all seven of us rushed Mad Dog. Mad Dog set himself as we charged. I don't know what we looked like to Mad Dog, but we must have been a sight because as soon as he set himself he bolted like a jack rabbit down the row back to C Cottage.

We heard a whistle and turned around as Brother Matthew called us back into our cottage giving each one of us a high-five hand slap for sticking together.

He told us that, "Together, we can stand; but alone, we would fall." He told us to clean our rooms, wash ourselves, and get ready for dinner.

Pepe and I took a shower and put on clean clothes. We were cleaning our room and I was still unpacking when we heard Brother Matthew's whistle.

"Line up for dinner," was announced.

My dad had packed my new suitcase with some new clothes, so I put on a new pair of Levi's with a blue plaid, short sleeve shirt and new blue Converse tennis shoes. I hadn't had a haircut since before the Camarillo nightmare, and I looked like the skinny little brother of Angela Davis with my big 'fro.' It felt good to wear clean new clothes, but boy did my face hurt! It was swollen so much that I couldn't open my mouth too far because of my busted and swollen bottom lip. My right eye was good and black now, and all red where it used to be white.

As we lined up for dinner, Brother Matthew checked our hands and made Jerry go wash his. Jerry was a nice kid, kind of overweight, smart as a whip, red hair, green eyes, and a face layered with freckles.

"Cleanliness is next to Godliness," Brother Matthew explained. "We are undoubtedly the smallest, but we will be tough, and we will always be the cleanest. Understood?"

"Yes Sir!" We all chimed in.

As we made our way out onto the row, E Cottage was right in front of our cottage. They already knew about the fight between Pepe and me, and were pointing and saying, "Whoa!"

I guessed that the 'backdoor grapevine' was how the news traveled so quickly.

King Al looked me dead in the eyes as he pointed to me, then Pepe, and growled, "At my table, you two and me are having dinner!"

I looked at Pepe, who had only two words to say, "Aw, shoot."

Our entire cottage was quiet as mice as we walked double file behind E Cottage. Jerry was behind me and whispered, "Nobody has dinner with King Al and lives to tell about it. It was nice meetin' yah!"

Pepe turned around and said, "Shut up, fat boy!" to which Jerry retorted, "If my lip was as fat as yours, I'd put it on a diet!"

A couple of the kids laughed.

CHAPTER 25: DINNER WITH THE KING

As we entered the cafeteria I thought, "Well, I didn't even make it to one meal before I got killed in Boys Town. Way to go, bright boy."

We grabbed our trays and got in line. Hamburgers, French fries, an ear of corn, and red Jell-O with a chocolate brownie and whipped cream were placed on my tray. Yummy.

Wow, I hadn't eaten since breakfast. Of course, it felt like we were in 150° heat except when we were inside the buildings, so maybe that killed my appetite. Plop went two cartons of milk on my tray and I followed the line toward the dining tables.

There was King Al motioning Pepe and me over to his 'Royal Table' where he, I guessed, sat alone unless he had 'invited guests.'

We sat down just as King Al finished his burger and was annihilating his French fries by the handful. Between handfuls of fries, he would squirt ketchup from a red bottle directly into that destructive machine he called a mouth.

I started to pick up my burger and, fast as lightning, King Al smacked me right on the knuckles with a spoon. Ooww!

With his other hand he grabbed my burger; and, with one huge machine-like bite, half my burger was gone.

Pepe tried to pick up his burger, too, and also received a quick rap on the knuckles with that same spoon. At the moment my burger disappeared into that dark void of a mouth, Pepe's burger was lifted from his plate by the huge hand of King Al. With a growl, King Al looked at Pepe and snarled, "Why did you get into a fight with Eddie? You know what I do to *cholos* who beat up on my people?"

Pepe squirmed in his chair as he watched remorsefully as his hamburger was being destroyed in this huge eating machine. One bite, two bites, three bites, gone! King Al licked mustard off his thumb and went to work on my French fries by the handful.

"Well?!" King Al demanded of Pepe.

"I'm sorry, King Al. I would never do anything to make you mad, but he called me Japanese!"

King Al's head went back and, with a mouthful of ketchup and French fries (mine were gone by now, and Pepe's were quickly disappearing), he let out a roar of laughter so loud that the whole cafeteria went quiet.

"You *do* look like a little Japanese!!! Look at your tight, little, slanted eyes! So *this* is why you want to beat up on my little bro??!!! You ###***!!!!"

From laughter to complete anger in a split second, all the while finishing Pepe's fries.

I reached for my brownie and received a smack of the spoon, but this time right square on my forehead! Ooowww!!

My brownie, King Al's brownie, and Pepe's brownie all met the same fate at the same time as Al swallowed them almost whole, three at a time. What an eating frenzy this gorging machine was accomplishing right in front of us.

I looked at my corn, but thought better of reaching for it; and good thing, too, because it left my plate via King Al's paw, entered his mouth whole and, after a twist or two, came out an empty cob. Gone. Finished. Sucked dry in two seconds.

Pepe's corn met the same fate, only faster, and King Al sucked down our Jell-O right out of the bowls, one right after another, including his own.

What Al did to those cartons of milk, all six, was beyond comprehension. Gone in seconds, King Al let out a burp so loud and so long that the cafeteria once again went instantly silent.

King Al sat back in his chair. He inserted a toothpick between his teeth as Pepe answered, "I wasn't going to fight him. I just wanted to scare him. He hit me first!"

King Al looked at me and said, "Is this true?"

"Yes, King Al," I said.

"Okay, so, Eddie, what do you want me to do to him, huh? Kill him, or what?"

"King Al, we're best friends now, please don't do anything to him. He's my friend," I pleaded.

King Al looked at both of us like we were so pitiful, so uncool, and too little to be any kind of threat to anyone. He just shook his head in dismay. Then, as he rose from the table, he let out a fart of humungous proportion and said, "Hey, really enjoyed dinner with you two dudes. Let's do it again." As he started to leave, he announced to the whole cafeteria, "I like these two dudes. Don't mess with them."

And King Al left the cafeteria.

Pepe let out a long sigh of relief as I looked over the mess King Al had made of his 'dinner table' in such a short time. I figured that, with my big lip, I probably wouldn't have enjoyed my burger anyway.

"Thanks for sticking up for me," Pepe said. "Man, we're celebrities. We lived through the Last Supper!"

Pepe explained that supper at the King's table was sometimes called the Last Supper because, while no violence might occur at the table itself, a verdict could be handed down in which the perpetrator would be sentenced and severely beaten up at another time. Very few had supper with the King and left the table without a verdict being handed down. We both became celebrities of sorts because the King proclaimed us as his friends when he said, "I like these two dudes."

High fives, free cigarettes, and great respect followed us for months because of this. The statement "Don't mess with them" was our key to the Kingdom. Unless Al revoked our status, or there was a change of Kingship, we had become 'hands off.' No one could touch us without having to answer to King Al.

Brother Matthew clapped his hands twice as a signal to line up and leave the cafeteria. We were led out of the cafeteria amidst remarks like "Way to go," and "Really cool, man," from the other cottages present. By the end of dinner, all cottages would have the word.

As we walked back over the hill, the teasing started. Brother Matthew asked me how I enjoyed my first dinner at Boys Town.

"It looked real tasty to me," I said, and everybody laughed.

Steve asked Pepe, "How was supper at the King's table?"

Pepe giggled and said, "He's got the fastest spoon in the west! And I believe that if I'd put ketchup on a sneaker, he'd have eaten it!"

Everyone laughed, and Jerry added, "And, yeah, then he'd let out a real wet and juicy fart and say thank you."

We were all in stitches, laughing so hard. Even Brother Matthew was roaring with laughter.

As I went to bed that first night in Boys Town of the Desert, in Beaumont, California, I thought, "Well, Mom, you really did your homework. I could very easily get killed in a place like this."

I promised myself that night that if I ever got out of here alive, I would surely one day pay my mother back for this.

What had I done to her that was so terrible that she could hate me enough to want me brutalized and possibly killed?

From Camarillo and the child molesters, to this—kiddie killers in a sand box. What was so wrong with me that I didn't deserve to live?

One day, I'd show her how to really, really hurt someone.

One day, I'd pay her back for everything she'd done to me.

One day, she would find out how I really felt about her.

One day, I'd get my revenge.

One day, she'd pay dearly. One day, ….

That night, as I struggled to drift off to sleep in my new surroundings, I quickly realized that Boys Town was the same as Camarillo in one important way: children crying themselves to sleep at night, screams in the middle of the night, nightmare after nightmare.

CHAPTER 26: CATCHING RATTLESNAKES

Boys Town of the Desert was an extremely hot place in the summer, and surprisingly cold in the winter. We had classes every day except weekends. We went to chapel every day and Mass on Sundays. We had P.E. (Physical Education) every day at the school for two hours, which was the highlight of each day. Baseball, football, and swimming were our main sports, during P.E..

At least once a week we got to go into town, either downtown Beaumont or sometimes Banning. If we won the cleanest cottage award, which we usually did, the prize was $50 and the keys to the flatbed truck to go into town. We could either buy clothes or go to the movies with our winnings.

Once or twice a week, Brother Matthew led us on a hike out into the desert, with 115° to 125° being the usual temperature range. One goal was to catch rattlesnakes since Brother Matthew knew a doctor in Beaumont who would buy the rattlesnake venom from us, and a store owner who would buy the skins as long as the rattle was still attached—$25 for each snake's venom, and $25 for the skin.

On the dirt paths, a rattlesnake might be coiled up asleep, basking in the sun; but, as soon as it felt the vibrations of our footsteps, it let out a warning by shaking its rattle. As we approached, there it would be, coiled up and hissing. With all that show, it proved to be easy to catch, and I don't remember ever *not* catching one.

On my first hike, I was the one who had to lose my T-shirt. Pepe was a master of this intense and dramatic final moment of a rattlesnake's life. As Pepe approached slowly, the snake really sounded off, flicking its tongue in and out of its mouth, and moving into its coiled position, ready to strike.

Pepe threw the T-shirt like a blanket over the snake which would, in turn, strike upward, leaving its coiled position and making a point in the T-shirt. The snake, with its head covered by the T-shirt, was blinded and, at that moment, Pepe would grasp the snake just below its head, then cut off its head with a sharp knife, leaving a bloody, messy hole in the T-shirt. Brother Matthew would press the snake's fangs against a glass vial and milk out the venom before corking and pocketing the vial.

Once that was done, we would search for a stick and a red ant mound. These red ants were called Army Ants or Fire Ants. We sliced open the snake's belly from rattle to neck, laid it out near the red ant hole, and came back a couple of days later to a perfectly cleaned snake skin. The ants cleaned all the meat off the skin, and I do mean *all* the meat. This skin was *perfect for a hatband or whatever else the store wanted to do* with it.

The stick? The T-shirt was put on it to mark the spot so we could find our skin again. Brother Matthew used a black marker pen to write Cottage A on it in case another cottage came past our ant hole.

This business of snake hunting gave our cottage more money for going to town. Brother Matthew also bought us treats for our cottage, like ice cream, cake for birthdays, pizza, cookies, and other snacks.

While we were hiking, we also caught and kept alive as pets horny toads and huge lizards.

It was normal to see a kid with a horny toad riding on his shoulder or a lizard in his shirt pocket. And nobody really cared if their "pet" ran away. There were a gazillion of them out there, they were easy to catch, and they hung around only long enough for a meal or two of fresh flies.

Brother Matthew taught us to respect and care for God's little creatures, and that torturing and/or killing these pets was a definite no-no!! That crime would probably get you killed and buried in the vast desert. I dunno, but nobody was stupid enough to do it.

CHAPTER 27: DRINKING POOL WATER

Going to town was great, but scary. After Brother Matthew lined us up in front of the cottage, we waited to see this old beat-up flatbed truck coming over the hill. It had no sides or rear gates, just a flatbed platform. Behind the cab or in the cab was the safest place to ride.

The road out of Boys Town was dirt and lots of potholes, so the ride was very bouncy. My greatest fear was falling off the truck and going underneath those big ugly wheels and being smashed into prairie dog snacks or vulture munch; but you couldn't let the other kids know you were scared or they'd either pretend to throw you off, or actually toss you overboard.

On one trip, we hit a dip so hard that one kid was thrown into another who fell off the truck and hit the back of his head so hard that he was in a coma for a week or two.

I hated the trip to town, but loved being in town. In Banning was the old campus: dismal gray and brick buildings, three and four stories tall, built probably in the 1920s. Brother Matthew sometimes took us there to swim.

Swimming was definitely last on my list of things to do while on earth. As a matter of fact, swimming became the top of my list of things not to do while I am on planet earth. I was exactly like a brick in water. A house brick. I was petrified to be in water that was over my head. I hated cold water except to drink. Besides, with my big old 'fro' and skinny build, I looked like a lollypop in swim shorts.

I hated swimming about as much as I hated my mother.

On bended knee, I begged Brother Matthew not to make me go swimming, or let the other kids throw me in the pool. Although he said I put together a great argument, he flatly refused to give in to my demands. He argued, "What if the boat you're in starts to sink?"

I promised him that I would never go near a boat.

He argued, "What if there's a flood? Like Noah's?"

I answered, "God promised not to do that again, right?"

Brother Matthew continued, "What if a dam breaks?"

"I'll stay indoors, upstairs, in a closet, under a blanket!"

I was doomed! Most of the time, it was the 8-handed sack toss entrance to the pool; but sometimes, the sneak-up-behind-and-push-really-hard approach was used. Although I hated both, the favorite seemed to be the 8-handed sack toss, with a kid on each hand, and one on each foot, swinging me back and forth before releasing me upward and outward toward the water. Down I would come, crashing into the water, screaming, kicking, and hollering, but to no avail. Most days, even after 20 tosses, they still weren't tired.

Then I guess they eventually got tired of this and taught me to swim. After about 10-15 minutes, I was able to dog paddle, swim on top of the water, swim under the water, and even do the butterfly. Pretty soon I was swimming on my back.

Still hated it, though. The water was always too cold, but I was glad they weren't throwing me in anymore.

I was no longer drinking pool water martinis!

CHAPTER 28: THE GHOST OF SISTER KELLY

Something unbelievable was going on at the old campus in Banning where we swam.

One night Brother Matthew got the truck and said, "We're going to visit Sister Kelly."

I asked Pepe, "Who's Sister Kelly?"

Pepe shook his head, and answered, "She's a ghost, man. She's a real ghost."

I looked straight at Pepe and said, "Sure, man!"

Jerry and Steve were at me quick with, "It's true! She's a real ghost. We've all seen her. You'll see."

As he was driving, Brother Matthew let me ride shotgun as he told me the story of Sister Kelly. Now, trust me, I'm thinking to myself, I don't believe in ghosts and can everybody be totally losing their minds? Even Brother Matthew?

He explained that the Catholic Church ran the old campus and both boys and girls went there. Sister Kelly was a nun who was also a teacher. As Sister Kelley went up some stairway to her class, she caught a boy and girl messing around, which was a serious offense. As she was leading them to something like a principal's office, one of them pushed her and she fell down the long flight of stone stairs and died. It happened on a Tuesday night, so Brother Matthew said that on every last Tuesday of the month, she would come out to haunt the old empty facility.

"Why would she haunt the place?" I asked.

Brother Matthew explained, "The other nuns took her stuff—her rosary, Bible, robes, and shoes. She won't leave until they're all brought back."

He told me that she tore up the kitchen one time, throwing pots and pans until the cook finally ran out of the kitchen. He was the same cook who cooks for us now in Beaumont at the new campus. I later verified this incident with him, and he confirmed it verbatim.

As we approached the old campus, the kids on the back of the truck started pounding on the roof of the cab shouting, "Look, there she is!"

Sure as I'm writing this story in ink, I saw her. Up on the roof of the first building on campus, which was the church, dancing in the moon light was a cloud, shaped just like a nun with the nun's hat and robe and all.

If I hadn't seen her with my own two eyes, there is no way I would have believed the story everyone was telling.

The Ghost of Sister Kelly.

Who'da thought?!

CHAPTER 29: SAMMY THE MOLESTER

Once, as we were leaving from an afternoon of swimming at the old Boys Town, King Al and his cottage of older boys were arriving. King Al slapped Pepe and me a high five without saying a word, as we walked by each other.

I was about to comment when one of the older kids named Sammy, whistled at Pepe or me like he was whistling at a girl. I said to Pepe, "Hey, did you hear that, what's up with that dude?"

Pepe elbowed me in the side and said, "Just keep walking. I'll tell you later."

Steve turned and looked at Pepe, then me, and then Jerry, and without a word, turned back around.

"What gives?" I asked.

"Shhh!!" Pepe said without looking at me.

When we got to the truck, Steve sat next to me and quietly said, "That was Sammy the Molester who whistled at you guys. He's raped every boy at Boys Town except for the guys in his cottage."

"What?!" I said, not believing what I was hearing. "And

he's still alive?" I asked.

Steve lowered his eyes and said quietly, "Who can beat him? He's big, we're small and besides, he's got a knife."

"Are you telling me we can't all take him?" I asked Pepe who just held his head down like a whipped pug.

"Everybody is scared of him," Jerry answered.

"What about telling Brother Bernard or Brother Matthew?" I asked.

Pepe answered, "Sammy cut up the last kid who tried to tell on him, real bad. The kid went to the hospital and never came back to Boys Town."

"That makes no sense to me. What about King Al?" I exclaimed in disbelief.

I found out that King Al and Sammy had apparently had more than one fight. On one occasion, King Al and Sammy fought almost to the death. King Al ended up getting cut and received 30 stitches in the hospital. King Al tried to take Sammy's head off and dislocated his jaw, so Sammy had to have his jaw wired.

On another occasion, they fought a grueling fight until

neither of them could raise their hands to block or throw another punch. The King Al Fan Club agreed that King Al won that fight. Sammy had no fans, although some said he might have won that fight because he was still standing at the end.

"So, what's happening with King Al?" I asked. "Can we still go to him if Sammy attacks us?"

Pepe looked pitiful as he quietly replied, "Us? Ain't no us. You're the only one Sammy hasn't gotten to."

I still couldn't believe what I was hearing, a child molester among us? Just like Camarillo, this place also had a sicko psycho. I just couldn't believe that Pepe, Steve, and Jerry had all been raped and never did anything about it. "This must be one bad rapist," I thought.

If King Al had trouble putting down Sammy the Rapist, what could I do if he came after me? After thinking about it for a while, I figured I'd rather die than get raped, so I'd fight him to the death if I had to.

Well, sure enough, Sammy the Rapist came after me. Our cottage was returning from a hike and, as we got about 100 feet away from the backdoor of our cottage, out came Sammy from a camouflaged hole.

All the other kids had run ahead to get at the water and bathrooms, and I was bringing up the rear. Sammy came up right beside me out of a pit covered with branches and leaves, and had a knife to my throat just like that. Fast as lightning he was.

"Say a word, and I'll kill you," he growled as he pushed me into his hole in the ground. "Well," I thought, "Now what do I do?" I could feel the sharp blade on my throat as he unloosened my pants, and pulled them down.

I said to myself, "No way is he going to put anything up in me," and even though the knife was still at my throat, I knew in my heart I'd rather be dead than raped by an almost grown man.

Sammy had to have been 20 or 21 years old. I was 13 or 14 and ready to kill or be killed by this sicko psycho. He tried to put it in me, but I squeezed so tightly that he couldn't. He then told me to turn around and suck him off. As I turned, I grabbed sand with both hands and threw it into his face, which caught him by surprise. His eyes were open when the sand hit his eyeballs, so all he could do was drop the knife, hit his knees, and reach for his eyes.

With a loud yell, I jumped out of the hole, fastened my

pants as fast as I could, and yelled toward the cottage for Pepe.

Still holding his eyes, Sammy screamed at me, "I'll kill you for this, you little half-breed!"

I screamed back at him, "Not today you won't, you weirdo!! And I will tell Brother Matthew on you!"

Running as fast as I could to the cottage, I left Sammy writhing in the hole.

I hurriedly led Brother Matthew and the other kids from my cottage back to the hole, Sammy's *stalking pit*. That sicko was nowhere to be found; but there, in the camouflaged hiding place, was Sammy's knife. The expressions on the faces of the boys peering into that hunting hole confirmed my story. It was Sammy's knife.

Brother Matthew immediately reported to Brother Bernard, filling him in on what had happened. They conducted a search for Sammy the Rapist and found him, his eyes still irritated and bloodshot from the sand.

You know, that day has haunted me all my life, because all I did was run. I had him at a disadvantage, and I could have kicked the snot out of him and broken his arms and half-way killed this sick kid molester. So many of his victims would have been rooting for his demise. I could have given all of them the satisfaction of knowing that someone stood up to him and really hurt him back for all his heinous crimes.

Justice would have been served that day. Instead, I ran. Like a scared rabbit, I ran. If I had taken that knife and cut off his member, he couldn't have hurt anyone else.

And you want to know what really haunts me? I wonder how many children he raped after that day in the hole. How many? He'd already raped 50. Did he rape another 50? Could I have saved them all that day? If I hadn't run?

I wish I could have written a different ending to this sad horror.

CHAPTER 30: GOING HOME

I remained in Boys Town until the late summer of 1970. Finally my parents, with my sister and brother, came again to get me. No, my mother never said a word all the way home. I had forgotten how much I hated her until she looked at me like I had no right to live on the same planet with her.

My brother and sister were acting weird, like they would be penalized for talking to me. Quieter than mice in a cat's house they were.

We stopped for burgers and shakes at an A&W Root Beer in San Bernardino, and I sat alone with my dad. I asked him why everyone was treating me like this. He said they hadn't seen me in a while, and that I was in serious need of a haircut. I had an Afro about 15 inches long in all directions. He said I looked like a militant, and that I would have to get it cut before I could go to school next week.

"School?" I asked. "What school?"

"High school. Lutheran High School," he told me. He said it was a fine private school and he didn't want me fighting or starting problems. My dad said these words to me, "If you don't get along this time with everyone in school and home, I just don't know what will happen to you or where you'll end up. So just ignore everyone and keep to yourself and you'll be all right."

He also told me that my mom was angry that I was coming home, and warned me not to say anything to her. She had also told my brother and sister all the way there in the car not to grow up like me, not to be like me, not to talk like me, to stay away from me, and don't even talk *to* me.

My mom never said a word to me the whole time I was in high school. Four years, not a word. Plenty of mean, ugly looks, but not one word.

When we got home, I finally met Queenie. Wow! She was the most beautiful German Shepherd I'd ever seen. She was big and intimidating to look at. I knelt down about 15 feet away from her as she looked at me. I called her and she slowly came to me. As she came close I offered my hand for her to smell. She did, and offered her neck for me to rub. We became friends instantly. My dad was right when he had told me that she loved to play. Boy! Did she love to play! I played with her every day before and after school. Because of my love for Mitzi, I was a little reluctant to fall in love with Queenie. Deep down inside, I did not want to love another dog. But Queenie quite rapidly stole my heart. She would run alongside me as I rode my bike through our neighborhood. She loved to play go-and-fetch-it with a tennis ball I had found for her. I would brush her coat every day. She was a fabulous dog and my best friend.

At 15, I entered 9th grade at Lutheran High School. I'd never heard of the school. All of my old friends went to Dorsey High or Crenshaw High.

"Friends" isn't a good choice of words. Better to label them as neighbors and old elementary school classmates. To be truthful, I had no friends.

High School was so different from being locked up. These kids were actually happy. Can you believe it? Happy kids. I kept my mouth shut and just watched them, listened to the way they talked and what they talked about.

I was so afraid of not fitting in or of making a wrong statement and giving away my background. There was no way I could let these nice, fine, and well brought up kids know that I had been in a nuthouse and then a place like juvenile hall.

We had chapel every day just like at Boys Town. It was also very similar to the Catholic service. The difference being that these kids actually looked like they cared and were really praying.

The freshman football coach saw me and told me he wanted me to play football for him. He asked me what position I wanted to play. I told him quarterback, running back, or split end. I really was good, but never got the chance to show it. I was really good at street football and playing all day at the park. You'd think these kids in the park were a lot tougher. And I really excelled at both football and baseball at Boys Town.

I had fair speed, excellent hands, and super moves. My dad said yes that night at dinner and filled out the paperwork. He even handed me a check to give my coach in the morning.

After dinner, my dad took me to buy some football cleats. I told him how much I liked the school and asked him if he would come to the games. He said he was too busy for that and to just have a good time and stay out of trouble.

"Keep your nose clean!" was what he used to say to me. "Just keep your nose clean."

I believe it meant to stay out of trouble.

CHAPTER 31: MAKING FRIENDS AT LUTHERAN HIGH

The nicest thing about making friends at Lutheran High was that these really were nice kids. They were helpful and giving and just plain nice. This was something that I was just not used to. Except for Clark, Darrell, and Pepe, I had never really had a friend.

There were of course, kids I had played with at the park and in the neighborhood. One boy in particular was the son of a man who was friends with my dad. They were a nice family, the Wrights, and lived a couple of blocks from us. Their son Clinton loved football as I did, and we played catch in the streets, or in their backyard.

At Lutheran, I met another boy named Wendell Greer. He also lived in my neighborhood and we became great friends. He was nice, easy going, and funny—a really nice kid from a nice family. We hit it off immediately.

Wendell and I both made the freshman football team and even rode the bus together after school to get home. He was really smart and helped me a lot with my studies.

I watched how he related to others and I copied him for

the most part. Transitioning from Boys Town to Lutheran High was no easy task, especially if you didn't want anyone to know your past. I didn't want this secret to get out so I never told anyone; but I had to fit in so that no one would be suspicious of my past. A couple of kids had actually come from Audubon Junior High as I had claimed, but said they didn't remember me. I just prayed that it wouldn't backfire on me later.

Although I made friends easily, there were not that many pretty girls. Most of the good-looking girls were already spoken for by the "jocks," so girls were pretty much ignoring me those four years. Oh, there were quite a few that I had crushes on. They just didn't know that I was enrolled in their school. I even talked to one or two of them, or at least tried. They would just look at me as if to say, "Oh, I *know* you didn't just walk over here and form your little lips to speak to me!!!" or "Could you leave as fast as you got here??!!! You're weird!!!!" or "You couldn't even imagine in that feeble little thing you call a brain that I would even entertain the thought of going out with you!!! Go away!!! Get away from me!!"

Rejected by every single good-looking girl, I at least had made some good friendships with fellow ballplayers and classmates—but they were guys!!

It was the girls I was after. Wendell felt that if we could get in with the right circle of guys, we might increase our chances of meeting some beautiful girls. Wendell, as you might guess, was having about as much luck with girls as I was having. None!!!

We became friends with Presley Burroughs and Ed Potter. Like us, Presley liked to fish, plus he was a brainiac, so we figured girls would line up to him for help with their homework. Yeah, right! He was doing worse than I was with the girls. "Not a chance" was the league we were in!

Now Ed Potter was a different story. He was one of my more interesting friends. He was so cool that he once had an awkward moment on purpose just to experience it! Not only a big, tall, good-looking guy, Ed was a protector of the meek. He chased away bullies. It is me we are talking about him defending, and he came to my rescue a bunch of times. There were only a couple of bullies, but they sure wanted to pick on me for some strange reason.

Now Ed played tennis, so he brought two more friends into the equation: Greg Bowles and Greg Malone, and they had two of the best girls on campus. Wow!! Now we're getting somewhere! *Not!!* The two Gregs held on to their girls, couldn't care less that we had none, and didn't do a thing to help our dilemma.

We were hopeless—so we concentrated on cars, sports, and fishing.

Me getting a girlfriend was like fighting a flood with a spoon!

It just wasn't going to happen!

A losing battle!

Forget about it!

CHAPTER 32: GRADUATING LUTHERAN HIGH

High school was pretty uneventful. I did manage to stay out of trouble. No fighting. No dating. Boring.

During my senior year, I met a girl from Fairfax High. Her name was Doris Anderson. She kissed me and I fell in love. She just seemed to love everything about me. I sure loved everything about her. My dad had bought a car for me, so I tried to see her every day after school.

She asked me one day to take her to my house. She wanted to see where I lived. I hadn't told her about my mom.

When we got there, Mom wasn't at home, so I gave her a grand tour of the Wiggins Estate.

My brother was in our bedroom studying and my sister, who was being picked up by Mom, hadn't gotten home yet.

My little sister was ten years old, so cute, and smart as a whip. Like my brother, she was also a straight "A" student. She often sat beside me in my room while I put together models. I installed lights and motors in a lot of them, so I proudly showed her all my models and the different things they could do. She was my only fan. I believe we were closer than my brother and I ever got.

From her bedroom window, she watched me play basketball in the backyard. I always waved at her when I saw her. When my friends from school or the neighborhood came over to shoot baskets, they would spot her in her window and ask, "Who's that?"

I simply replied, "That's my little sister, and don't even think about it."

After showing Doris my home, I took her into the backyard and kissed her really good before we started to do our homework together. As we sat really close together on the patio, doing our studies at the table, my mother came home. She looked at us and said loudly, "Get this *tramp* out of my backyard!"

I felt so bad. Doris was really hurt and cried as we got in my car and left. I felt like a heel. Why had I brought her here anyway? I should have just told her no when she asked to see where I lived. Now Mom had insulted, and deeply hurt, the only person I loved besides my dad and brother and sister.

We never went back to my house again. I had to explain to Doris that the problem wasn't her; it was my mom. I had to reveal to her my childhood and all the horrors I had gone through. Doris cried while she listened. When I was finished, she asked me, "What is wrong with your mom?"

"I don't know, my love. She has always hated me."

Doris came from a wonderful, loving family. I really liked her family. Mr. and Mrs. Anderson were so nice and friendly. They were so understanding and loving. Doris also had an older sister, La Tricia who was a real sweetheart. La Tricia had two boys, Craig and Tony. Nice kids who both loved football. Every time we'd go over there, I'd play with them in the front yard. Mr. Anderson would sit on the front porch and talk to me about his life, and give me good advice.

Mama Anderson, as everyone called her was just the sweetest Mom on earth. And she could cook! Boy could she cook! There was always something good cooking in her kitchen. Whenever I went over to Doris' house, my first stop after kissing the love of my life, was the kitchen. I would kiss Mama Anderson on the cheek and say, "What are you cooking, Mama Anderson? It sure smells good!"

"I'm cooking corned beef and cabbage. Have you ever had it?"

She cooked a lot of things that I had never eaten, like greens and cornbread, neck bones with gravy and rice. Her catfish would knock your socks off! She made the best fried chicken, and made sure I tried everything, opening up a new world of dining that I had never experienced.

We all became very close. They had a wonderful family and made me a part of it with welcoming arms. I could talk to Mama Anderson about anything. She also taught me about her church and how God wants us all to be healed and told me things about God that I had never heard. She loved telling me about "hands on healing."

Not knowing God personally or having a personal relationship with Jesus, I had a tough time relating to these things she was teaching me. I didn't really believe that God would give us power to heal the sick. It was enjoyable to listen to her, though, as she projected a confidence in her beliefs and the way Jesus worked in people's lives.

I think what really excited me about the Andersons was that they liked me, for me. Mama Anderson had become like a mother to me. I loved her and she loved me more. I loved being around them. They didn't judge or condemn anyone. They just helped and loved everyone.

Doris' dad, Louis Anderson, was one of the nicest men I had ever met. He was on the quiet side; but when he spoke, he was a fountain of wisdom. He was retired from the railroad and about to retire from the phone company. Boy! Could he tell you some real-life stories: people he had met, places he had seen. Louis was a very gentle, awesomely knowledgeable man.

I would often tell Doris how wonderful her family was. Doris and I were inseparable. We went everywhere together, except school. We would spend hours kissing. Boy, oh, boy! Could she kiss!

Getting back to Lutheran High School, there really isn't a lot to tell. I never really excelled at anything. I graduated with a 3.4 grade average, and, with the nickname of Mr. Flat, I sang in our *Acapella* choir. I was in the band and attempted to play clarinet, saxophone, drums, and xylophone—all with no success. Maybe because I hated them all!

I really never put my heart into football or baseball either. The coaches had different ideas about where to play me, and I never got to play where I wanted, so sports really became just something fun to do instead of something to go after seriously.

I made a lot of good friends, had a lot of fun, met a lot of nice families.

Then I had to go home.

CHAPTER 33: NEARING THE EDGE

My mother was still not speaking to me unless she had something hurtful or hateful to say. It was nice, however, to have met the Andersons, to just know that there were good people and nice families that existed.

I still hated my mother and I seemed to hardly exist to the rest of my family. Except for the Andersons, I had no idea what it felt like to have a 'loving family, and, when I had to go home, I was left feeling cheated, empty, and wondering what had happened to make my family the way it was. Although I had made many friends in high school, they didn't know the real me. They still didn't know what I had been through or how I really felt deep inside. I was still seething inside, but I held it in, not wanting to share my burden, not wanting to risk more rejection for just being myself.

I still had no personal relationship with Christ Jesus, and no clue as to how I was supposed to feel and act. I was so lost, so lonely and so weak when it came to the things of God. I really wondered a lot if God truly existed. If He did, did He even know about me? Mrs. Anderson tried to share her relationship with Christ with me, but He was never real to me then. I was too mixed up inside. How could God be real and let all this madness exist? I had no idea that Jesus was there the whole time protecting me, shielding me, keeping me alive for a day such as today.

God had a purpose for me, but I was clueless about that purpose because I was too busy searching for who I was and how I was supposed to fit in to this weird and crazy world. I wanted to be liked and loved and to love, but I never seemed to fit in, to find my place, to excel at anything. I always seemed to lack in everything. I seemed to not even think like others. I seemed to have no purpose, except to be a punching bag for those who were stronger.

I had no clue who I was, why I was here, where I was headed. I floated along, like a log in a river being knocked against the rocks and the shore. Just there.

What would I do with my life?

Where would I go?

Who would really love me for me?

Would I ever get the chance to really love someone?

What would I become in the future?

Would I eventually let out all of this hate inside me and kill my mother? All I wanted was to be as far away from her as

220

possible.

What lesson did I learn about myself? Well, I learned that if you want to create a mixed-up kid like me, abuse them beyond belief!!

So much goes on in the lives of a youth like me. There needs to be an outlet. I really had no one to talk to except the Andersons, and I would share only so much. I tried to be a good listener, but could not absorb what Mrs. Anderson tried to tell me. I just bumbled around, taking on the worst blows that life had to offer. What was life all about, anyway? Should I really care? I needed someone to talk to who could hear my whole story, someone to listen to the grisly details and my heartache, someone who could make me feel safe, someone who could free these thoughts and feelings from inside of me. Maybe then I could know some peace.

I thought about joining the Marines and going to Vietnam, certainly not because I loved to fight, but because I loved flying and had a fascination with being able to leave the earth and fly in the peacefulness of the sky. I used to watch planes and helicopters fly, and I marveled at what it must be like to be up there. Was there freedom up there? Was there peace up there? Would I find myself in the skies above the earth? Being down here was not all it was cracked up to be. I had found no real satisfaction being here on earth. Perhaps I would be happy in the sky.

During my last year in high school, I went to the Marine recruiter's office and took the test. There was a draft at that time, but I had missed it by a couple hundred numbers. I qualified for Officers Candidate School, which meant I could come out as a Second Lieutenant. I took the physical and passed. I filled out nearly all the paperwork and had nothing left to do except graduate high school and then sign the last paper.

I imagined flying amongst the clouds and finding peace while being separated from this earth. I imagined the peace I might find there, and that my rage and hatred against my mom might float away into the clouds. But I also imagined the reality of killing enemies I did not know. I didn't like that idea, but perhaps I could handle that if I pretended that each one of them was my mother! Maybe *that* would release my hatred! Hmm…. Hope they have really big guns!! And give me lots of them!

Three days before I was to graduate high school, I had a terrible dream.

My goal was to fly the Harrier, a jet fighter aircraft that can take off and land like a helicopter. I loved this plane so much that I used to wear out the recruiter by asking for literature and colored pictures, and to watch the recruitment films of this beautiful plane. In my dream, I was sitting on my helmet in a Huey UH-1B. There was shooting going on and a bullet came through the bottom of the helicopter, right through my helmet, and hit me. I saw myself die a slow, painful, horrible death. And I could have sworn that a voice told me, "If you go, *you will die!*"

I woke up in a sweat, scared to death! I wanted to learn to fly, but I was not willing to die for it; so my new plan was to go to college and study aerospace engineering. Perhaps I could fly in the private sector.

Truly, I had no clue what I wanted to be in life. Everything I did was out of reaction, not decision; self defense, not self-advancement; survival, not personal knowledge or direction.

I trusted no one, especially grown-ups, who I found to be greedy and dangerous. They would lie to you in a second. Sure, I knew there were a few good folks, but basically I just could not bring myself to trust anyone. I had seen too much, heard too much, and been hurt too much.

I hated what I saw in this world. The way people treated

each other. Books in school projected life one way; but, in reality, all I could see was dog-eat-dog. How could I make things better for myself?

What I really wanted to see just did not exist, or at least I could not find it. Peace, love, gentleness, people being honest and fair. I thought that, in America, all of your dreams could come true. That's what I had read. What I witnessed, however, was a different story. It was everyone out for themselves. The way I thought the world *should* be was not how it truly was. I had enough hate, anger, pain, and loneliness to last a lifetime.

This was a horrible reality for a child as naive as I was. How *empty* I felt. Where would I fit in? *How* would I fit in? Would I *ever* fit in?

Now you're asking yourself, "You mean it just keeps going? When do we get to the *good* part?"

Not soon enough, my friend. Not soon enough....

CHAPTER 34: IS THIS THE END?

Well, this might seem to be where my story ends, but my story has actually barely begun.

In my next book, I describe in detail, holding nothing back, my thirty-one years of getting high on drugs. I'll expose most of what I saw, did, and experienced in the drug world during those three decades.

If you have gotten high before, you will understand better the traps I fell into; however, if you have *never* been high, this will be the unveiling of another world—a dark one.

If you want to keep your children, friends or loved ones off drugs, my next book will definitely scare them away.

I call it *The Syndrome*—everything they didn't tell you when they handed you that first joint and said, "Try it, you'll like it!"

I will also tell of the miracles that God did through me and for me. In case you have not heard my testimony, Jesus really did take me to hell. I saw it, I felt it. I will share it all with you in *The Syndrome*. My testimony will also be released in another book that will be available soon, *To Hell and Back*. My mission in life is to tell the world, especially the churches, that hell is real, and we do not have to go. Jesus died on that rugged cross to make sure that none of us would have to go.

By His blood, we are saved.

By His Stripes, we are already healed!!

Rev. Eddie with his oldest son, Dr. Edward T. Wiggins II

Rev. Eddie with his youngest son, Lee,
a U. S. Navy Seabee

Lee, dressed and ready for Afghanistan

Angelina and Gilbert
I love you both so very much

Other Books Coming Soon by Rev. Eddie

To Hell and Back

The Syndrome

Out of the Dark and into the Light- from Death to Life

Three Girls and Two Boys

The Adventures of Rev. Wilson- Angel

The Adventures of Rev. Wilson- The Prayer That Touched God's Heart

The Adventures of Rev. Wilson- "Angel and Goliath"

A Young Man's Conversation with Jesus